FOUL DEEDS & SUSPICIOUS DEATHS IN SOUTH YORKSHIRE

TRUE CRIME FROM WHARNCLIFFE
Foul Deeds and Suspicious Deaths Series

Barking, Dagenham & Chadwell Heath	Jersey
Barnet, Finchley and Hendon	Leeds
Barnsley	Leicester
Bath	Lewisham and Deptford
Bedford	Liverpool
Birmingham	London's East End
Black Country	London's West End
Blackburn and Hyndburn	Manchester
Bolton	Mansfield
Bradford	More Foul Deeds Birmingham
Brighton	More Foul Deeds Chesterfield
Bristol	More Foul Deeds Wakefield
Cambridge	Newcastle
Carlisle	Newport
Chesterfield	Norfolk
Colchester	Northampton
Cotswolds, The	Nottingham
Coventry	Oxfordshire
Croydon	Pontefract and Castleford
Derby	Portsmouth
Dublin	Rotherham
Durham	Scunthorpe
Ealing	Shrewsbury and Around Shropshire
Fens, In and Around	Southampton
Folkstone and Dover	Southend-on-Sea
Grimsby	Staffordshire and The Potteries
Guernsey	Stratford and South Warwickshire
Guildford	Tees
Halifax	Uxbridge
Hampstead, Holborn and St Pancras	Warwickshire
Huddersfield	Wigan
Hull	York

OTHER TRUE CRIME BOOKS FROM WHARNCLIFFE

A-Z of London Murders, The	Norwich Murders
A-Z of Yorkshire Murders, The	Plot to Kill Lloyd George
Black Barnsley	Romford Outrage
Brighton Crime and Vice 1800-2000	Strangeways Hanged
Crafty Crooks and Conmen	Unsolved Murders in Victorian &
Durham Executions	Edwardian London
Essex Murders	Unsolved London Murders
Executions & Hangings in Newcastle	Unsolved Norfolk Murders
and Morpeth	Unsolved Yorkshire Murders
Great Hoaxers, Artful Fakers and	Warwickshire's Murderous Women
Cheating Charlatans	Yorkshire Hangmen
Norfolk Mayhem and Murder	Yorkshire's Murderous Women

Please contact us via any of the methods below for more information or a catalogue
WHARNCLIFFE BOOKS
47 Church Street, Barnsley, South Yorkshire, S70 2AS
Tel: 01226 734555 • 734222 • Fax: 01226 734438
email: enquiries@pen-and-sword.co.uk
website: www.wharncliffebooks.co.uk

Foul Deeds & Suspicious Deaths in

SOUTH YORKSHIRE

GEOFFREY HOWSE

This book is Dedicated in fondest memory
of my cousin
STEPHEN CLIFFORD WILLOUGHBY
1950-1979

First Published in Great Britain in 2010 by
Wharncliffe Local History
an imprint of
Pen and Sword Books Ltd
47 Church Street
Barnsley
South Yorkshire
S70 2AS

Copyright © Geoffrey Howse 2010

ISBN: 978-184563-103-1

The right of Geoffrey Howse to be identified as author of
this work has been asserted by him in accordance with the
Copyright, Designs and Patents Act 1988.

A CIP catalogue record for this book is available from the
British Library.

Typeset in Plantin by Concept, Huddersfield.

Printed and bound in England by the MPG Books Group.

Pen & Sword Books Ltd incorporates the Imprints of
Pen & Sword Aviation, Pen & Sword Maritime,
Pen & Sword Military, Wharncliffe Local History,
Pen & Sword Select, Pen & Sword Military Classics,
Leo Cooper, Remember When, Seaforth Publishing and
Frontline Publishing.

For a complete list of Pen & Sword titles please contact
PEN & SWORD BOOKS LIMITED
47 Church Street
Barnsley
South Yorkshire
S70 2BR
England
E-mail: enquiries@pen-and-sword.co.uk
Website: www.pen-and-sword.co.uk

Contents

Acknowledgments

Iris Ackroyd, Keith Atack, Vera Atack, Michael Barber, Susan Barber, the staff at Barnsley Central Library Local Studies Department, Joan Bostwick, Giles Brearley, Robert Alan (Bob) Dale, Kathleen Dale, Iris Deller, Joanna C Murray Deller, Ricky S Deller, Tracy P Deller, Gary Dulson, Brian Elliott, Doug Hindmarch, Senior Local Studies Librarian at Sheffield Central Library and the staff at Sheffield Central Library, Ann Howse, Doreen Howse, Kathleen Howse, Brendan E McNally, Pamela Mott, Eleanor Nelder, Stanley Nelder, Adam R Walker, Anna Walker, Christine Walker, Darren J Walker, David Walker Emma C Walker, Ivan P Walker, Paula L Walker, Polly R Walker, Suki B Walker, Thomas A Walker, Clifford Willoughby, Margaret Willoughby, Ken Wyatt, Roy Young and I am particularly grateful to John D Murray who has assisted me over many years.

Introduction

ong before the creation in 1974 of the short lived South Yorkshire County Council, there had been an area within the West Riding referred to as South Yorkshire. There has never been a South Riding – except in the eponymous work by Winifred Holtby, published in 1936, the year after her death – because riding means 'a third part of', and historically Yorkshire's ridings have been the East, North and West.

Today, the modern county of South Yorkshire is divided into four major urban areas: the metropolitan boroughs of Barnsley, Doncaster, Rotherham and Sheffield. The principal towns and cities all have a rich history, but many smaller towns and villages within South Yorkshire have interesting histories, in some cases of greater significance in the affairs of the entire country. South Yorkshire, that centuries old enclave in the historic West Riding,

Conspiracy. Author's collection

has over the years seen many a foul deed committed within its boundaries. I have attempted to include a broad cross section of foul deeds from comparatively trivial crimes to the ultimate crime of murder, spanning the years between the reign of William IV and the 1950s. With regard to the wealth of crime history material available within South Yorkshire I have barely scratched the surface, or indeed moved beyond the tip of the proverbial iceberg. However, in an effort to provide the reader with as wide a breadth of foul deeds as possible, in as many different districts I have delved into countless documents and old newspapers in order to enable me to include some seriously disturbing cases as well as some lighter and more quirky crimes.

It is interesting to compare how the scales of justice worked in years gone by to deal with felons and petty criminals and those involved in crimes of violence, to the penalties imposed in today's courts. Sometimes, or indeed one might almost say, more often than not, extreme poverty was at the root of crime and there is many a sad story to be told. Standards of morality, social prejudices and a person's position within society all played their part with respect to the commission of crime and the administration of justice. Simply to be poor, was tantamount to some less charitably disposed both in thought and deed, to amount to being part of the criminal fraternity. Magistrates did not always deal fairly with miscreants, and sometimes what today seem inordinately harsh sentences were handed down for seemingly trivial crimes or indeed relative misdemeanours.

In writing this, my eighth True Crime title, I have tried to provide an interesting and accurate account based on available documentary evidence. I apologise unreservedly for any errors or omissions.

Chapter 1

A Miscellany of Crime from the Reign of William IV to Queen Victoria

The Swell Mob at Doncaster, 1834

... assured of a valuable booty, the three men determined to appropriate it for their own use on the last day of their visit.

On 6 October 1834, *The Times* wrote an article concerning the goings on at Doncaster's famous September Race Week:

> *Doncaster, which at the season of the great St. Leger race is at all times the scene of desperate speculations, presented one at the meeting of a daring and successful description.*

The report went on to say that on the first day of the race meeting three men of respectable appearance, dressed in the first style of fashion, went to the *Falcon Inn*, where they made inquiries about the availability of beds and other accommodation throughout the week. There being space available to accommodate these gentlemen, they were duly booked in, and their luggage conveyed to their respective apartments. *The Times* said this about the three gentlemen:

> *Their manners indicated a disposition to give freely, and to sustain the character which they had assumed. They ate and drank of the best, and expense seemed to be the last consideration in their minds. They every day visited the race course, with the apparent curiosity of strangers, and it was concluded that they were young men of fortune, who had no other pursuit, but that of pleasure. In the end, however, it turned out they were playing a deeper game.*

The men paid particular attention to the movements of their host and discovered that he not only presided over their comforts at the *Falcon Inn* but also had a refreshment booth on the racecourse, to which a large body of people resorted during the course of each day's racing. They also observed that after each day's racing was over, their host, on his return from his booth, took the day's receipts to what he believed to be a secure room upstairs in the inn. Thus assured of a valuable booty, the three men determined to appropriate it for their own use on the last day of their visit. To that end they managed to remove their own luggage, with the assistance of two others, to another house. While two of the men prepared to avail themselves of the landlord's money, the third kept watch from the road outside, of the window that looked from the landlord's room. Meanwhile, the two men inside gained entry to the room where the landlord's valuables were kept, and broke open an escritoire, stealing more than £100. While the men were at their business, the landlord decided to visit his chamber, but upon finding some resistance when he attempted to open the door, supposed that some of his female intimates of the house were there, returning again downstairs. The two men inside being somewhat alarmed, decided to effect their escape by means of a window, the drop from which was not great. When the landlord returned downstairs he made inquiry of his servants as to which of his family was in his upstairs chamber. On being informed that none of them were, the landlord quickly returned upstairs, only to discover his loss, and that the 'birds had flown'. The landlord looked out of the window just in time to see his three generous customers running off into the distance.

Gaoled for Shooting Gamekeeper, Wath-upon-Dearne, 1864

... the other poacher was striking Broadhead with a hedge stake and the other fellow swore he would knock his brains out with another bludgeon.

William Broadhead was on duty in Low Wood at Wath-upon-Dearne, when he saw three men, of whom the prisoner was one, engaged in ferreting for rabbits. Broadhead went up to Moxon and placed his hand on his shoulder, upon which the prisoner and a second fellow not in custody commenced beating him over the head with a hedge stake. Broadhead and Moxon then struggled for the possession of Broadhead's gun, which was double-barrelled and at half cock. The poachers subsequently kicked Broadhead over the hands and stamped all over them, and at length Moxon

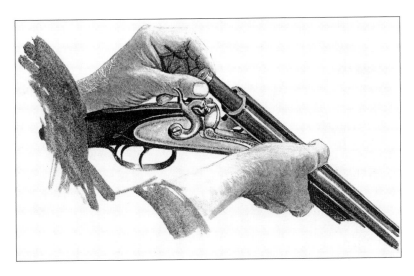

got hold of the stock of the gun, the barrels being then directed at Broadhead. The struggle lasted about a quarter of an hour, and the prisoner during the greater part of the time had his hand on the trigger, after having pulled up both the hammers.

Broadhead was laid upon his back when Moxon pulled the gun forward a little, and discharged one barrel. The charge of heavy shot, fortunately for the gamekeeper, went into the bank upon which he was lying, and just missed his side. Moxon and the other poacher then got possession of the gun, and Moxon pointed the gun at Broadhead, who cried out:

For God's sake don't shoot me.

That being said, the prisoner then uttered an oath and declared he would 'blow him through', then made an effort to let off the other barrel, which had a defective trigger end upon it. While this was going on the other poacher was striking Broadhead with a hedge stake and the other fellow swore he would knock his brains out with another bludgeon. Broadhead prayed that they would not take his life, upon which they asked him if he intended to follow them up, to which he replied that he would not if they didn't kill him, and then they backed away into the wood, keeping their faces towards him in an attempt to intimidate him from following them. But Moxon was in the act of crossing the fence, having one hand on the back trigger and the other half way down the barrel. The left hand barrel, which had become stuffed with mud during the struggle, suddenly exploded, and the gun appeared to jump out of Moxon's hands. The three poachers then concealed themselves in the wood. Broadhead subsequently ascertained that both the barrels of his gun had burst.

The assistant to Dr Clarke of Wentworth, said that the prisoner went to the surgery on 4 June, saying that he had got his right hand hurt whilst shooting at small birds, the barrel of his gun having burst. The prisoner was subsequently sent to Sheffield Infirmary, where he was identified by Broadhead as the man who had shot at him, and he was also spoken of by several witnesses as having been seen on the Wentworth Road shortly after the struggle in the company of three other men. The description of Moxon's clothing, furnished by these independent witnesses exactly tallied with the articles of clothing found in the prisoner's home.

At his trial at the Assizes, Moxon, who was undefended, declared that the wound was caused by the bursting of his own gun, nine weeks previously, whilst shooting at birds in his own garden. After a brief consultation the jury found Moxon guilty. His Lordship told the prisoner:

> *You are one of those men who beginning simply by what was called poaching, had gone on until you got into a crime as serious as that which you have now been convicted. If the shot had taken effect, as I much fear you intended, you would have been standing on trial for your life, and if a similar verdict had been returned I would have been obliged to send you for execution. The expressions that were used by yourself and your fellow poachers were of the most shameful kind and the keeper was treated very disgracefully. This case is one of a most serious character and I cannot sentence you to a lower sentence than four years' penal servitude.*

Shocking Assault and Robbery, Barnburgh, February 1867

It is impossible to pass an offence of this kind over without a very severe punishment, for it is worse than robbery on the highway.

On the morning of Saturday 9 February 1867, a widow, Elizabeth Dawson, living at a small farm at Barnburgh, near Doncaster, was in her bedroom, when her attention was drawn by the barking of her dog in the kitchen. She went downstairs to see why the dog was barking and as she entered the kitchen she saw a man at the kitchen door. She asked him what was his business, and he said he had come to ask her to let him spread some manure over one of her fields. She told the man that she had given the job to another man by the name of Marshall. He then asked for a drop of beer, which Mrs Dawson gave him, and the man kept her in conversation for about twenty minutes, with the purpose, it is believed, to ascertain if there was anyone else present in the house. The man continued with his conversation, and, having satisfied himself that Mrs Dawson was alone, when she asked him to leave, he threw himself upon her, and seized her by the shoulders, forcing her into the middle of the kitchen. He then demanded her money. Mrs

Charles Lister assaulting widow Mrs Elizabeth Dawson at her farmhouse at Barnburgh. Illustrated Police News

Dawson said she had no money, but he threatened her to such an extent that she handed him her purse, containing seven half-sovereigns, two half-crowns and several groats (silver fourpenny pieces). The man then knocked her down on the floor, and, taking a knife or razor out of his pocket, he drew it across her throat without touching her; and when she let out a scream for help, he dragged her to the cellar head and threw her down a flight of thirteen steps.

The man then took to his heels and proceeded to jump from whence he had come, where he saw his sweetheart and gave her three guineas of the money he had stolen, to prepare for their wedding, which had been arranged for the following Monday. Meanwhile, Mrs Dawson remained in an insensible condition in the cellar and when she came round, she found that her assailant had fastened her in. A fourteen-year-old youth who called at Mrs Dawson's house heard her calls for help. He entered the house and located where the noise was coming from, then unlocked the cellar door and freed Mrs Dawson, who was severely injured. The police were summoned and medical help was sent for.

A man answering the culprit's description had been seen in the vicinity and the police were soon hot on his trail, which led them to one Charles Lister, of Jump, and on Friday 15 February he was brought up before West Riding magistrates Dr Scholfield and Sir Issac Morley, at Doncaster's Guild Hall. Charles Lister was a tall, rough-looking fellow, and he stood in the dock charged with having violently assaulted and robbed Mrs Elizabeth Dawson.

During the course of the proceedings:

> Sir Isaac Morley: *I should like to ask whether there was anyone in the house at the time.*
> Mrs Dawson, replied: *No.*
> Sir Isaac: *Where was the servant?*
> Mrs Dawson: *I don't keep one.*
> Mr Astwood: *The house is a very lone one, and lays some distance from the road.*

The Bench decided that there was sufficient evidence against the accused and he was committed to take his trial at the Assizes.

On Friday 29 March, Lister's case was heard before Mr Justice Lush.

Jane Hodgson, of Jump, said she was engaged to the prisoner and on 9 February she met him at Elsecar, between five and six o'clock in the evening when he gave her about £3, of which part was in silver and the rest comprised four half-sovereigns. John Battersby, a fourteen-year-old youth, of Barnburgh, said he was near Mrs Dawson's house at eleven o'clock on the morning the attack took place. He heard her calling out and he was able to release her from the cellar. She was very shaken and was severely wounded.

Mr Blytheman, surgeon, stated that Mrs Dawson had sustained very serious injuries from violence and from being confined in a damp atmosphere. The whole of Mrs Dawson's spine was in a contused state, from the neck downward. The lower part of her body was very much swollen, the right side being black and double the natural size, caused by some blow that she had received.

The jury found the prisoner guilty. When addressing Lister, His Lordship told him:

> *In my opinion this is a very bad case indeed. I do not know when I have heard a worse case. To think that a lonely woman, living in a lonely house, in a quiet neighbourhood, should be assaulted by such a ruffian as yourself, in that manner seems almost incredible, and especially that being so near a village. That you should have inflicted such injuries that the poor woman will suffer from them during the remainder of her days. It is impossible to pass an offence of this kind over without a very severe punishment, for it is worse than robbery on the highway.*

His Lordship then passed sentence, giving Lister ten years' penal servitude.

Two Lovely Black Eyes, Assault at Doncaster, May 1867

Black struck him a violent blow between the eyes, the force of which knocked Mr Grayson off his feet and he fell to the ground.

Joseph Black, described as being a respectable looking resident of Hexthorpe, was brought up before the Mayor, H Woodmansey, Esquire, the Ex Mayor, R E Clark, Esquire and Sir Isaac Morley, at the Guild Hall, Doncaster, on Friday 31 May 1867, charged with having assaulted another Hexthorpe resident, William Grayson, a carter.

An early twentieth-century view of St Sepulchre Gate, Doncaster. Old Barnsley

Mr Grayson appeared in the witness box with two black eyes.
The Bench heard that on Saturday 25 May, Mr Grayson was
coming down St Thomas Street with his daughter. He was having
a few words with her and, when they arrived at St Sepulchre Gate,
they met Joseph Black, who took it upon himself to interfere
between father and daughter. When Mr Grayson expressed his
displeasure at such effrontery, Black struck him a violent blow
between the eyes, the force of which knocked Mr Grayson off his
feet and he fell to the ground. After hearing the evidence the
Mayor said that Black had no business to interfere and should not
have struck Mr Grayson. Joseph Black was given a fine of 5*s* and
ordered to pay costs.

Assault on the Highway, Thurgoland, January 1868

*... Haigh came up and knocked him down, whereupon
Morley kicked him in a brutal manner ...*

Charles Haigh, Thomas Morley, John Smith and William Jackson
were charged with assaulting David Barraclough on Sunday

5 January 1868, at Thurgoland, when they appeared before W S Stanhope, Esquire and the Rev H B Cooke at Barnsley Court House, on Wednesday 15 January. Mr Freeman of Huddersfield defended all four men. The Bench heard that the four defendants and Mr Barraclough were drinking at the *Rock Inn*, Crane Moor, during the evening and until late on Saturday 4 January. At about midnight they were all turned out. A while later a fight ensued between Mr Barraclough's brother and Charles Haigh, in a field, at Thurgoland. Charles Haigh separated the two men, and his brother departed the scene and Mr Barraclough then set off on his way home. All four defendants followed him and Haigh came up and knocked him down, whereupon Morley kicked him in a brutal manner, before Smith and Jackson joined in the assault. For the defence, Mr Freeman contended that David Barraclough and Charles Haigh had agreed to fight and that none of the others interfered. Having considered the evidence the Bench fined Haigh 5*s* and costs. The three other defendants were discharged.

Sheep Stealing at Darfield, February 1868

... found pieces of mutton that had been cut from the body in an unskilful manner ...

John Latham farmed 150 acres at Darfield. On Saturday 1 February 1868, he had 307 sheep on his farm, and on 4 February, having purchased some more stock, fifty additional sheep had been added to his herd. The following morning one of the herd was missing, and a while later in a pasture about 100 yards from the field where the herd was kept, a sheepskin was found, which bore the marks of the missing animal. Circumstantial evidence led police to the home of two colliers, Luke Williams and William Baker, who lived together. There they found pieces of mutton that had been cut from the body in an unskilful manner, and some of these pieces exactly fitted the skin of the missing animal, found in the pasture. Footprints at the scene also provided evidence against Williams and Baker. At the West Riding Assizes, before Mr Justice Hannan, on Saturday 28 March, the two men were found guilty of killing a sheep with intent to steal the carcass. Williams was sentenced to four months' imprisonment with hard labour, and Baker to six months' imprisonment with hard labour.

Stack-firing at Brinsworth, December 1868

As I find this crime is very rife in this part of the country any one who is found guilty of it before me I shall consider it my duty to punish very severely.

Milk-dealer George Thompson owned land in the parish of Brinsworth, where during the late summer of 1868, one particular pasture field had been mown and the hay stacked on the spot. At about two o'clock on the afternoon of Sunday 8 November, twenty-two-year-old, collier Samuel Hall and thirty-eight-year-old tailor Adam Henderson, were seen in the pasture field, walking towards the haystack, by a woman, who lived about 100 yards away. Within minutes the woman noticed the haystack was on fire and she hurried to inform Mr Thompson, the stack's owner. Both Hall and Henderson were subsequently taken into custody, where-upon each tried to throw the blame on the other. Henderson said:

> *We had been in Sheffield Workhouse all night, and when we were coming past the stack, I said, 'It's damned cold, would you like to have a heat?' Hall said, 'Aye hast thou a match?' I said I had. I gave him one, and he struck it on his breeches and set fire to the stack.*

Hall, on having heard Henderson make this statement, replied:

> *You are as bad a man, for you lighted the match.*

Hall and Henderson were duly committed by Rotherham magistrates to take their trial at the Assizes, where the jury found both men guilty. The judge was moved to comment that the prisoners were that sort who usually commit arson. It transpired that in January 1867, Hall was convicted of stealing a coat, and in October 1867, he was convicted of stealing another coat. One might assume from this and also the desire to keep warm by setting fire to Mr Thompson's haystack, that Samuel Hall, was particularly averse to cold weather conditions. In October 1868, he had spent a month in prison for destroying clothes when he was in a workhouse. Henderson had spent one month in prison earlier that year for disorderly conduct in a workhouse and also another month for destroying clothing in a workhouse. The judge went on to say that evidently both men would not work to get an honest livelihood, and when put into the workhouse would not live quietly at the expense of the public, and when they came out, through nothing but a feeling of envy and hatred against everybody in better circumstances than themselves, they wilfully set to work to destroy other people's property.

In this particular instance Hall and Henderson did not know the victim of their actions. They could have no ill-feeling towards him, yet they had done that which would cause a loss to Mr Thompson of about £50. His Lordship then added:

> *As I find this crime is very rife in this part of the country any one who is found guilty of it before me I shall consider it my duty to punish very severely.*

Having made this statement, he then sentenced Hall and Henderson to seven years' penal servitude, respectively.

Garrotte Robbery at Sheffield, January 1869
... grasped him by the throat and brought his head down to the ground, rendering him semi-conscious and virtually incapable of struggling.

On 11 January 1869, William Wright was about his business as a traveller in the employ of Sheffield cornmillers Samuel Smith and Co. As part of his duties Mr Wright went about the town and neighbouring towns and villages collecting money and orders. He habitually went to particular districts on certain days. On this particular day Wright had been out from ten o'clock in the morning until six o'clock in the evening, having collected the sum of £404 during his business dealings. About £90 of this money was in gold and silver and was in his trousers pockets. At about six o'clock, as he proceeded down Netherthorpe Street, Wright was attacked by three men. There were several witnesses. One of Mr Wright's assailants grasped him by the throat and brought his head down to the ground, rendering him semi-conscious and virtually incapable of struggling, perpetrating a crime which had become known throughout England as a garrotte robbery. A second man held Mr Wright's arms, whilst a third robbed him of £72 7s 6d. The men quickly fled the scene, leaving him on the ground and they were not apprehended until several days afterwards.

Twenty-nine-year-old Thomas Hubbard, thirty-two-year-old William Hubbard and thirty-four-year-old John Gillbank, all railway spring makers, were brought up before Sheffield magistrates, who committed them to take their trial at the Assizes. On Wednesday 24 March, they were tried at the West Riding Assizes, before Baron Cleasby. Mr Barker prosecuted. Only Gillbank was defended, and he had Mr Tennant to speak for him. Several witnesses agreed in their statements that the three men in the dock were the same as those seen following Mr Wright. The two Hubbards vehemently denied they had anything to do with the matter and as proof that they were not involved in the robbery, they reminded the jury that they were not defended, which they said would not have been the case had they had any of the stolen money. The Hubbards maintained they were working in the town at the time they were apprehended, which would not have been the case had they been involved in the robbery, as they would have left the town as soon as possible. In Gillbank's defence, Mr Tennant said the principal witness had sworn to another man at the police station, though she subsequently withdrew what she said and pointed out Gillbank as being the man she had seen with the other prisoners and she had witnessed the attack from beginning to end. Others either saw Mr Wright being followed or saw his attackers as they fled the scene.

Having carefully summed up the evidence, Baron Cleasby asked the jury to consider their verdict against the three accused men. They returned a verdict of guilty against all three. The judge said he would have to consider the sentence, which it was his duty to pass. Thomas and William Hubbard and John Gillbank were brought up for sentencing the following day. His Lordship said:

There can be no doubt whatever that the robbery was a planned one, and that it had been planned for some considerable time. You at length thought that the time had come when you could carry it into effect as there was no one in sight of you and Mr Wright, except one young woman, who gave her evidence yesterday, and whose evidence, has in fact, convicted you. People are entitled to use a highway without any obstruction, and most of all, without danger to their lives, when they used them for the purpose of their business, and had valuable property in their possession. During the interval which has elapsed since your conviction I have considered whether in your case I can refuse to execute the power permitted to myself and other judges to punish such a crime as yours in an unusual manner; I have not found that any of you have up to the present time pursued a life of crime, and therefore I shall dispense with that mode of punishment . . .

Having said these words, His Lordship told the three prisoners he would sentence them to five years' penal servitude.

Engine Fitter Cuts Wife's Throat, Rawmarsh, February 1869

... instead of avoiding your greatest enemy you placed yourself entirely in its power, and under its influence committed the dreadful crime of which you have been found guilty.

On Monday 1 February 1869, twenty-seven-year-old engine fitter John Saxon Lyon, of Rawmarsh, appeared before magistrates at Rotherham Police Court, charged with cutting and wounding his wife, Eliza, on Sunday evening. The Bench heard that the prisoner had been on bad terms with his wife for some time. John and Eliza Lyon had lived in Rawmarsh for the past twelve months, with their two children, the husband being employed at works near New York. About ten o'clock on Sunday morning Lyon left home for Rotherham in order to pick up a parcel, which had been left behind during a visit to the market on Saturday night. He did not return home until some time between seven and eight o'clock in the evening and he was in a state of intoxication. An argument ensued about the husband's failure to bring the parcel home, and Lyon was heard by neighbours to say he would be the death of his wife. The argument continued and Lyon, who had a knife in his hand, began to attack his spouse. After a brief struggle Mrs Lyon managed to make her escape to a neighbour's house, where she collapsed in a chair, with blood trickling from a wound to her throat. Mr Smith, a surgeon, of Parkgate, was sent for. Her wound having been dressed, Eliza Lyon was taken to her mother's house in Hollybush. The police were informed of the incident and Police Sergeant Horne, assisted by Police Constable Hobson, went to Lyon's house to arrest him. When they arrived they found the door was locked and bolted. They later discovered that Lyon had retired to bed with his two children. The police knocked Lyon up but he refused to open the door and it became necessary to break in through a window in order to arrest him. Although Lyon professed to know nothing of the incident, a bloodstained Spanish clasp knife was found in his possession. Lyon was taken from Rawmarsh to Rotherham and locked in the police cells. Police Superintendent Gillett asked magistrates for a remand in custody, which was granted. Mrs Lyon could not appear in court for the initial hearing, as she was suffering from a puncture wound to the neck. After several appearances before magistrates Lyon was committed to take his trial at the Assizes.

On Thursday 20 March, Lyon was tried at the West Riding Assizes, before Baron Cleasby, charged with maliciously wounding his wife, Eliza, with intent to do her grievous bodily harm, by cutting her in the throat. Having heard the evidence of several witnesses the jury found Lyon guilty as charged. On Saturday 22 March, John Lyon appeared before His Lordship for sentencing. His Lordship told Lyon:

You are a man who witnesses have given a remarkably good character. Nevertheless, instead of avoiding your greatest enemy you placed yourself entirely in its power, and under its influence committed the dreadful crime of which you have been found guilty. This is not the first time you have got into some trouble on account of giving way to drink. However, as all the witnesses have spoken in your favour, your wife, upon whom the offence was committed, amongst the rest, I will not pass upon you a very severe sentence. At the same time, it is impossible to pass over such a crime as yours, without a punishment of some severity . . .

Having said these words, His Lordship passed a sentence upon Lyon of fifteen months' imprisonment with hard labour.

Wife Beater Lynched at Holmes, January 1869

He had scarcely left the entrance gates to the works when he was pounced upon by several of his fellow workmen . . .

On 23 January 1869 the *Illustrated Police News* reported an incident that had occurred in the suburb of Holmes near Rotherham. The *Sheffield and Rotherham Independent*, reporting on the same event, said the inhabitants of that pleasant suburb were determined a high standard of domestic morality should be maintained. One particular newly married young man, who was employed at one of the local works, was singled out for the local public's attention when it was discovered that he had inflicted corporal punishment on the young woman he had only weeks before sworn to love and protect. Such an early manifestation of wife-beating propensities was too much to bear for the tender hearted residents of Holmes,

A young wife-beater is subjected to the wrath of the mob at Holmes. *Illustrated Police News*

who at once formed a secret society for the purpose of avenging the wrongs of the injured wife. On Monday 18 January, the young man finished his day's work and set off on his journey home. He had scarcely left the entrance gates to the works when he was pounced upon by several of his fellow workmen and before he knew what was happening he was hoisted upon a rail, which did not provide a very comfortable seat. Several men took it upon themselves to ensure that the young man did not fall from his perch and went to great pains to maintain his centre of gravity on the rail, to prevent his falling and hurting himself. Thus positioned, the young wife beater was borne in mock triumph through the principal street of Holmes, preceded by a large mob of several hundred men, women and children, some bearing lighted torches and others beating cans and kettles, creating what newspaper reports described as 'a most unearthly din'.

In order that there could be no mistake as to the purpose of this demonstration of mass indignation, a board upon which had been neatly painted 'Wife-beater', was carried at the head of the procession. The affair caused great excitement throughout the whole neighbourhood, the women in particular working themselves into a state of great fury against the elevated ruffian. The procession ended its noisy journey opposite the *Pigeon Cote Inn*, where the young man was set at liberty, after which, it was said, he went home a sadder and wiser man.

Five Years for Post Office Robberies, Sheffield and Rotherham, February 1869

It is impossible to exaggerate the importance to society of the trust which was placed in you being faithfully observed.

On Thursday 19 March 1869, twenty-year-old clerk George Hague, who had previously pleaded guilty to stealing a post letter containing an order for £6 12s, at Sheffield, on 21 February, and twenty-three-year-old clerk Thomas Scarle, who had also pleaded guilty to stealing several letters containing valuable securities at Rotherham, were brought up in the dock to receive sentence at the West Riding Assizes before Baron Cleasby. His Lordship told the two prisoners:

> . . . the cases charged against you are not ordinary ones. You have been placed in a position of confidence by the Government of the country, and that confidence you have betrayed. It is impossible to exaggerate the importance to society of the trust which was placed in you being faithfully observed. Persons are dependent upon the regularity of their letters being delivered for their comfort and for perhaps their means of subsistence. I should have been glad in consequence of your previous good character or other circumstances to pass upon you a lenient sentence; but the interests of society and the claims of justice make it impossible to deal with such cases but with the utmost severity.

Having delivered his admonishment, his Lordship went on to sentence Hague and Searle each to five years' penal servitude.

Trade Outrage, Holmes, 1870

. . . the union were of the opinion that he was not entitled to engage men for brickmaking purposes.

Master brickmaker Thomas Slack, residing at Attercliffe, had employed for some time two men to make bricks on land situated at Holmes, near Rotherham. A few days prior to this outrage occurring, two men from the Brickmakers' Union visited Mr Slack and requested that he should discharge the men, as the union were

Thomas Slack's brickworks under attack during the trade outrages at Holmes.
Illustrated Police News

of the opinion that he was not entitled to engage men for brick-making purposes. They also informed him that before he could be considered by the union a person competent to act as a master brickmaker, he must serve two years as a kind of journey-man apprentice. Slack refused to discharge the men from his employment, or become an apprentice, he being fifty-two years of age. However, the two union representatives were not impressed by Mr Slack's comments and told him if he did not discharge the men '. . . he would hear more about it.'

In consequence of this unveiled threat Mr Slack made arrange-ments for the brickworks to be watched. And all was left well on Saturday at midnight. On the early morning of Sunday 17 April, sometime between four and six o'clock, new bricks were trampled upon and entirely destroyed.

Election Riots at Barnsley, 1874

... attempts were made to drive the mob out of the Market Place, the throwing of stones increased ...

On 11 February 1874 *The Times* reported:

> *Riots. – At Barnsley yesterday the excitement arising out of the election for the South-West Riding found vent in a rather serious tumult. During the hours of polling the town was tolerably quiet, with the exception of a few youths who amused themselves by pushing each other about. Towards 5 o'clock their rough play increased to throwing of stones, hampers, oranges and earthenware of all descriptions at the police ...*

At the Conservative headquarters in the *King's Head Hotel*, stones were thrown through the windows. When a short while afterwards attempts were made to drive the mob out of the Market Place, the throwing of stones increased and the windows of the *Coach and Horses Hotel*, *White Hart Hotel*, *Duke of York Hotel*, *Trafalgar Hotel*, *Wharncliffe Hotel*, *Victoria Hotel* and several other leading public houses and shops all received damage, estimated to exceed £150. Several police officers received serious injuries. A cab containing ballot boxes from the Hoyland district was attacked in Sheffield Road, its windows broken and a police officer injured.

Brutal Kicking at Bolton-upon-Dearne, Boxing Day, 1874

Padley struck him with something hard on the back of the head, knocking him to the ground.

On Saturday 9 January 1875, six young men were charged with assaulting Godfrey Hollingworth, the manager of Manvers Main Colliery and the Bench at Doncaster West Riding Court looked on the affair as a very savage and brutal assault. Henry Swallow, William Padley, Edward Swallow, Joseph Flint and Henry Bailey, all colliers, and labourer James Cooke, were involved. Apparently the men took offence to Godfrey Hollingworth because he did not mix with them socially. On Christmas Day Mr Hollingworth met two of the men at the *Angel Inn*, Bolton-upon-Dearne, and because they were ordered out of the room in which he was allowed to remain, they threatened to 'warn' him. On Boxing Day, Mr Hollingworth called at the *Angel Inn* again, and after partaking of a drink started off for home. He was followed by Joseph Flint and Henry Swallow, and, when Mr Hollingworth asked them why they were following him, they said they had come to 'warm' his head; and shortly after this exchange of words the other defendants appeared. Mr Hollingworth quickly took to his heels and ran home, with all the defendants in persuit.

It became necessary for Mr Hollingworth to go out for some purpose, and for protection he took a staff with him. However, Mr Hollingworth had scarcely got out of his door, when William Padley struck him with something hard on the back of the head, knocking him to the ground. Padley then urged the others to kick Mr Hollingworth, while he was down on the ground, and Bailey told them to 'go into him'. Cooke remarked that that was the man who had thrashed him some while ago, but he would give it him while he was down. All the men, with the exception of Padley, kicked Mr Hollingworth and he became insensible. While his assailants fled the scene a neighbour assisted him into his house. The next morning Dr Burnham was sent for.

Dr Burnham found Mr Hollingworth was bruised on the body, head, and face. There was also a mark on his forehead and his hip; and his arms and legs had also sustained serious injuries. The Bench heard that Hollingworth's injuries were so serious that he had only been able to work for part of two days since the attack took place. Witnesses were called to substantiate this fact. One of them, Mrs Bishey, said she prevented one man from ill-using Mr Hollingworth, and when Cooke was about to inflict further injury, she told him if he did not desist she would fight him herself. The Bench warmly complemented Mrs Bishey for her conduct. Mr Aldam remarked if there were more women like her many of these savage assaults would not take place.

In defence of the assailants the Bench heard that Hollingworth had brought it all on himself by his provocation. In the case of Bailey and Padley, an attempt at an alibi was made. The Bench said that if the defence had not attempted to show these mitigating circumstances, they would have sent five of the defendants to prison. William Padley and Henry Swallow were each fined £3. Edward Swallow, Joseph Flint and James Cooke were fined £2 each, and Henry Bailey was discharged.

Attempted Murder and Suicide, Sheffield, February 1875

... having returned with a six-barrelled revolver, which he pointed at his wife's head, and, without uttering a word, fired it.

James Margerrison, a forty-eight-year-old slate merchant, formerly a publican, lived with his wife and three daughters in well-to-do circumstances in Sheffield, Mr Margerrison possessing considerable property in the town. For three weeks before these tragic events occurred, he had been drinking heavily and he was seldom in his proper senses. On Friday 5 February 1875 he was away from home for the greater part of the day, returning at about eight o'clock in the evening in an intoxicated condition. On returning home he went immediately upstairs, saying that he was going to bed. His wife remained seated by the fire in the drawing room. Within minutes James Margerrison was downstairs again, having returned with a six-barrelled revolver, which he pointed at his wife's head, and, without uttering a word, fired it.

The bullet struck Mrs Margerrison in the face and passed through her mouth, knocking out three of her teeth. Margerrison then retired to the parlour, and placing the revolver into his mouth, fired the weapon again, falling to the ground. Despite her own injuries, his wife rushed to his assistance, and raised him from the floor. Mary Ann Walton, the Margerrison's charwoman, who had witnessed the whole affair, went to fetch assistance, and the house was soon surrounded by a great crowd.

The Margerrisons had three daughters. One of them, the eighteen-year-old, returned home just then having been out to make some purchases at the butcher's shop. She went into the parlour and was confronted by her father lying on the floor, with his head raised on her mother's lap, who with blood streaming from her mouth and tears from her eyes, was rendering what comfort she could to her prostrate and unconscious husband, who was oblivious to his wife's ministrations. The neighbours came in and placed him on the sofa. Medical help was quick to arrive and both Mr and Mrs Margerrison received attention. James Margerrison died within two hours. His wife recovered from her injuries.

There was unmistakeable proof that Margerrison had premeditated something of the kind. He had only recently purchased the revolver and the day before the fatal event he had made his will. Drink was supposed to be the cause of the outrage.

Indecent Assault on an Imbecile, Dodworth, July 1875

... Lister called in for a glass of beer and subsequently committed the assault in the bar parlour.

George Lister, a farmer living at Dodworth, appeared at Barnsley Town Hall on Monday 5 July 1875 before magistrates E Newman, Esquire and F Taylor, Esquire, charged with an indecent assault upon a forty-two-year-old 'imbecile', Ruth Gledhill. The Bench heard that Miss Gledhill was a resident of Higham Common. Her brother was the landlord of a public house there called the *Hermit Inn*, which was where the assault took place on Friday 2 July. On that day Miss Gledhill was about her business doing some cleaning at the inn when Lister called in for a glass of beer and subsequently committed the assault in the bar parlour. Several witnesses were called and their evidence resulted in the Bench sentencing Lister to a month's imprisonment.

Cannibalism at Rotherham, July 1876

... seized hold of Ellis's head with both hands and knocked it several times on the curbstone ...

On the evening of Monday 19 June 1876, John Pearce, of Masborough, appeared at Rotherham Police Court, charged with seriously assaulting Edward Ellis. Magistrates heard that on 7 June the two men were drinking together at a Masborough public house. Pearce said that Ellis made a remark about his wife which he regarded as an insult. Shortly afterwards Ellis left and boarded a lorry which was waiting outside. As he took his seat on the lorry, Pearce, who had followed Ellis, struck him on the head, the force of the blow knocking him from the lorry onto the ground. Pearce immediately seized hold of Ellis's head with both hands and knocked it several times on the curbstone, inflicting three severe scalp wounds. Apparently not content with that, Pearce bit one of Ellis's ears and also one of his hands. The resultant injuries following this attack necessitated Ellis being confined to hospital

John Peace bites a chunk out of Edward Ellis's ear, at Masborough. Illustrated Police News

until Saturday 24 June. Pearce was found guilty as charged and fined £5 or in default one month's imprisonment.

A Darfield Gentleman Sent to Gaol, November 1876

... he got hold of my middle finger with his teeth, my finger end was bit about quite through the nail.

On Wednesday 1 November 1876, the none appearance in court at Barnsley Town Hall, of a gentleman, one John Townend Machen, Esquire, of Newhall, Darfield, did not go well for him. Machen's failure to appear on a charge of assaulting an ostler, James Weatherhogg, at the *King's Head Hotel*, on the night of Friday 29 September, resulted in him receiving a prison sentence. Magistrates T E Taylor, Esquire, J Kaye, Esquire and J C Milner, Esquire, heard the case in Machen's absence.

After James Weatherhogg was called and sworn, he told the Bench:

I am head ostler at the King's Head Hotel. *I remember Friday night, the 29th of September. I was in the* King's Head *yard at eleven o'clock. It was my business to lock up the stables. I had only Machen's horse there. It was left during the afternoon. I had told Mr Machen to be in good time, as sometimes he did not come for his horse until morning. He turned up at ten minutes past eleven. He came in with Mr Hynings at about a quarter-past eleven. I told him he was just in time, as I was going to bed the horse down. I put on the saddle and bridle, and then proceeded to lead the horse out. As I was leading it out he shoved back both me and the horse twice. He then got hold of me and started to 'worry' me with his fists. I got out to the yard, where we had a scuffle, and then I ran into the street. It was in the stable when he first struck. He got hold of me in the yard, and struck me there, but I managed to get out of his way. He ran after me and caught me in the centre of the street. I called out for a policeman. He got hold of me round the neck, and tried to 'pay' me with his fists. I tried to get myself loose and in so doing he got hold of my middle finger with his teeth, my finger end was bit about quite through the nail. I got away, but not before I was bitten on the other hand . . .*

Weatherhogg then described how he had called out for the police and, on going back to the yards at the *King's Head Hotel*, saw Machen mounted on his horse. He was holding a long prop, shod with iron at the thick end, in his hand, with which he had already dealt Weatherhogg a blow. Weatherhogg shut and barred the door, fastening Machen in the yard. Weatherhogg remained on the outside of the door, preventing Machen from leaving, and instructed the hotel boots to fetch the police. Meanwhile, Machen remained mounted, as Weatherhogg could clearly see the prop, evidently intended to again use as a weapon, protruding above the gap at the top of the door. The boots returned shortly afterwards with three policemen. Weatherhogg said:

. . . I then opened the door. I picked up the prop and showed it to Inspector Stott. I then gave the defendant in charge. I then went to Mr Blackburn's to get my hands dressed. I brought Anthony Stryran back with me. I had put the horse back in the stable by the order of Inspector Stott, before going to the doctor. I would get back at about a quarter to twelve. Defendant, Mr Hynings, and Mr Wainwright's assistant

[Mr Dyer] *were there. Mr Machen wanted his horse. I told him I had been requested by the policeman to detain it. He offered to tie one hand behind him, and hit me with the other. He did not, however, strike me. I went into the stable and he went away. I did not see Hynings the whole time, he went away soon after coming into the yard. I did not see him again until I had returned from the doctor. There was no one with me in the yard when defendant came the first time. He did not come out of the house. In the stable I struck defendant after he had struck me. I struck only in self defence, in knocking his blow off.*

Several witnesses confirmed Weatherhogg's version of events. Mr Freeman called Henry Edmund Dyer, assistant to the surgeon, Mr Blackburn. After confirming that Weatherhogg was perfectly sober when he received medical attention, Mr Dyer said:

I first saw Mr Weatherhogg at about eleven o'clock on Friday night and he showed me a serious wound on his scalp. There was effusion which had run down his coat collar. There were contusions under the eye and a wound on the leg. The wounds on the leg might have been caused by a kick. The scalp wound must have been caused by a sharp instrument such as a poker. There were also abrasions on the upper and

John Townend Machen Esquire assaulting ostler James Weatherhogg, at the King's Hotel, *Darfield. Illustrated Police News*

lower lips. The eyes were much swollen and might have been caused by a blow with a fist.

After deliberating in private the magistrates returned and the chairman, Mr Taylor, said:

We have given this case a very attentive hearing and have come to the conclusion that it is clearly proved to our satisfaction. We shall commit Joseph Townend Machen to the Wakefield House of Correction to hard labour for one month, the sentence to take affect from the date of his apprehension.

Attempted Wife Murder at Rotherham, October 1876

Next to murder, as your learned counsel has most truly said, there is no graver crime than attempting to commit murder.

On Wednesday 13 December 1876, twenty-four-year-old colliery fitter James Breach, appeared before Mr Justice Hawkins, at Leeds Winter Assizes, indicted for feloniously shooting at his wife with intent to kill her. Mr Thomas appeared for the prosecution and Mr Tindal Atkinson defended the prisoner. The Court heard that the couple had married the previous March and since then Breach had left his wife to earn her own living. On 30 October he returned home after a long absence, and deliberately arming himself with a pistol and ammunition, went to the *Dusty Miller Inn* where his wife was employed. On entering the inn and seeing his wife Breach pulled the pistol from out of his pocket, pointed the weapon at his wife, and pulled the trigger. The weapon failed to fire and several people pounced on Breach, preventing him taking out a second loaded pistol, which he had concealed in another pocket.

The prisoner was followed by a large crowd to the police station, where some of the crowd called out that he ought to be hanged, to which the prisoner replied:

I wished I had shot the ★★★★

Mr Tindal Atkinson in defending the prisoner tried to show that Breach could not have intended to kill his wife, as the powder with which the pistol was loaded was so coarse that it would never reach the nipper. The jury were not impressed by this submission and found the prisoner guilty. Mr Justice Hawkins, addressing Breach, said:

> It was a merciful intervention of Providence which prevented that pistol from going off and causing the death of your wife. If that pistol had gone off, and if, as a consequence, your wife had been killed, you would have stood there to receive sentence of death, and most assuredly you would have died for the crime of murder. Next to murder, as your learned counsel has most truly said, there is no graver crime than attempting to commit murder. Now that the jury have prosecuted their verdict in this case, I am at liberty to express my own opinion, which entirely coincides with the view they have taken. I have not a shadow of doubt, when I look at all the circumstances of this case, that you went to this public house, having prepared yourself with two pistols in the event of one not being effective, for the purpose of accomplishing the deadly object you had in view. Crime like yours must be punished with exemplary severity. The punishment that I award to you is that you be kept in penal servitude for twenty years.

Manslaughter by Frying Pan, Sheffield, August 1877

... persons like yourself must be taught to restrain your violence.

On 24 August 1877, twenty-four-year-old miner Samuel Foster, of Sheffield, was in the throes of a heated argument with another man, when he took up a frying pan with which to hit him. Eliza Ann Oates, who was at the scene, was the unlucky recipient of the blow, which had missed its intended target. The force was such that it caused the young woman's death.

On Wednesday 10 April, Foster stood in the dock before Mr Justice Hawkins at Leeds Spring Assizes, having pleaded guilty to a charge of manslaughter. His Lordship, addressing Foster, said:

> I do not suppose for one single moment that you intended to inflict any injury upon the poor woman, whose death you caused; but still persons like yourself must be taught to restrain your violence. It was a brutal and wanton thing to take a weapon like a frying pan and strike at any one. If serious injury was so caused then consequences must be suffered.

His Lordship then ordered Foster to be imprisoned for eight months with hard labour.

Wife Burning at Sheffield, December 1877

I give you the benefit of believing that had you been in your sober senses, you would not have committed such an offence.

Forty-eight-year-old Irish labourer Thomas Flannaghan was apprehended by Sheffield police and charged with setting fire to his wife, Bridget, on the night of Saturday 8 December 1877. Bridget Flannaghan was found lying upon the bed, which was enveloped in flames, and her clothes were entirely burnt before she could be rescued. She was taken to the Infirmary in a critical condition, and by Monday such was the concern for her condition that it was necessary to take depositions at her bedside.

Mrs Flannaghan stated that a quarrel took place between herself and her husband in consequence of her refusing to give him some money. Because of Mrs Flannaghan's refusal, her husband told her that he would have her life, and set fire to her dress with a match, at the same time holding her down on the bed whilst her clothes and the bed clothes were burning.

Sheffield magistrates committed Thomas Flannaghan to take his trial at the Assizes. On Wednesday 10 April, Flannaghan was tried in the Crown Court at Leeds Spring Assizes, before Mr Justice Hawkins and found guilty of feloniously and maliciously causing grievous bodily harm to Bridget Flannaghan, his wife. In passing sentence His Lordship said:

> *You have been found guilty of setting fire to and burning your wife. You were not charged with setting fire to her with intent to murder, had that have the case then it would have been my duty to pass a much more severe sentence on you. The poor woman yet remains in hospital in a condition of great peril. Should she die, you will be liable to be tried for her death; and if it is found that death was as a result of injuries you inflicted upon her, you would be found guilty of murder; so even yet you might have to be put to death for your crime. You must not suppose that the punishment which is about to be inflicted on you will exonerate from the possibility of any further punishment. I advise you to pray earnestly that your wife might be restored to health for her own sake and for your sake also.*

His Lordship went on to say that the prisoner went into the house where his wife was lying asleep on the bed, and because she

Thomas Flannaghan sets fire to his wife Bridget while she is in bed. Illustrated Police
News

would not supply him with money to get more drink, that he
deliberately beat her with a poker and set fire to her clothing, there
could be no doubt. It was fortunate for him that he had a neighbour who was resolute enough to force in the door and rescue the
poor woman. Mr Justice Hawkins continued:

> *I am loth to believe that a man in his sober senses, or unless his mind
> was taken from him, would perpetrate such an atrocious crime.
> Drunkeness, however, is not an excuse behind which anyone can
> shelter himself from the consequences of the crime he has committed; but
> still the fact that you were besodden with drink to some extent mitigated
> the atrocity of the intention. I give you the benefit of believing that had
> you been in your sober senses, you would not have committed such an
> offence; but still you must undergo a very considerable period of penal
> servitude. It is possible, however, if you behave yourself in the gaol in
> which you will be confined, you might get some portion of the sentence
> remitted.*

His Lordship then sentenced Flannaghan to twelve years' penal
servitude.

Brutal Outrage at Rotherham, February 1878

... brutally treated and ravished by each of the four men in turn.

On the night of 24 February 1878, four men attacked and ravished a young woman, Jane Esther Robinson, whilst she was on her way home. As she was walking along the road Miss Robinson was thrown down, brutally treated and ravished by each of the four men in turn. On Wednesday 10 April, twenty-nine-year-old collier John Senior and twenty-two-year-old labourer William Sides, having been found guilty at Leeds Spring Assizes, of committing rape upon Jane Robinson, were brought up to receive sentences.

Mr Justice Hawkins said:

> *To my mind the offence of which you have been found guilty is of great atrocity, and but for the good character you have previously borne would be visited with a very severe sentence. Within my recollection such offences have been punishable by death. It is a ferocious crime when committed single-handed, but it is much more serious when several persons have banded together and by their unprotected efforts have ravished an unprotected female. Under these circumstances I must pass a sentence notwithstanding your previous good character, which will be a warning to other persons of a similar nature.*

His Lordship then ordered that John Senior and William Sides should each be kept in penal servitude for ten years.

Officious Police Inspector, Rotherham, April 1878

... holding the dead child up by the shoulders, asked the distraught young woman if the child was hers.

On Monday 8 April 1878 the case of the Crown *v* Newton was heard before Mr Justice Hawkins at Leeds. The case was notable for disclosing the mode of eliciting evidence from suspected persons on the part of the police, which when revealed, received strong admonishment from His Lordship. The young woman, little more than a girl, concerned had been in one situation at Rotherham as a domestic servant for seven years, and had been confined under circumstances that induced her mistress to inform the police.

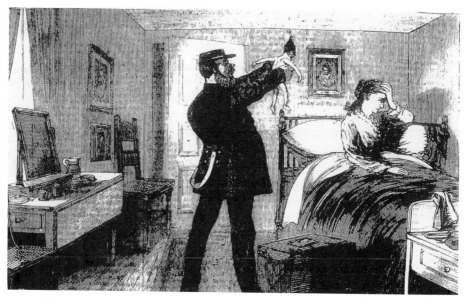

Police Inspector Parker holds up Miss Newton's dead baby, having removed it from the box in which it had been placed. Illustrated Police News

Inspector Parker went to the house, where he found Mr Knight, surgeon, and in consequence of a statement made to him, the Inspector went to the girl's bedroom, and questioned her as to what had taken place. The young woman gave no answer and the Inspector searched the room. He found the body of a new-born baby in a box. He removed the baby's body from the box and, holding the dead child up by the shoulders, asked the distraught young woman if the child was hers. She replied that it was, and the Inspector, under the instructions of the surgeon, removed the young woman to the police station in a cab, placing her in an ordinary cell.

His Lordship censured the officer for illegally questioning the woman, and gave indignation as to the conduct of the girl's mistress, the surgeon and Inspector Parker, in respect of her removal at the time. Happily the girl, Miss Newton, survived the treatment she received and the jury showed their sympathy by returning a verdict of not guilty, with an intimation of their approval of the remarks made by the judge. The general feeling was that the surgeon had exceeded his duty and the practice of questioning such poor creatures, in order to obtain evidence against them, an all too common occurrence, was as illegal as it was cruel.

Assault at Conisbrough, 1882

Appleyard then struck the lad on the side of the head with a shovel . . .

On Saturday 4 February 1882, farmer William Appleyard, of Conisbrough, was brought before the Bench at Doncaster Police Court, chaired by A Sturrock, Esquire, charged with assaulting his farm servant, Herbert Middleton. Herbert, a young lad, stated that at about six o'clock on the evening of Saturday 28 January, he was feeding the horses, when Mr Appleyard asked him why he had not taken the mare's collar off. Appleyard then struck the lad on the side of the head with a shovel, making his ear bleed considerably. Appleyard followed the injured lad to the stable and hit him again on the back. As the lad ran to the door, Appleyard tried to hit him again. Samuel Halliday was called as a witness but he did not see Appleyard hit the lad, only attempt to do so and fail.

In his own defence Appleyard said the boy was very saucy, and he had not unloosed the horses. He said through the boy's negligence he had lost a sack of barley, and had had a deal of trouble with him. Appleyard added the boy vexed him but he had not struck him. The magistrates did not believe Appleyard and said they were perfectly satisfied that an assault had taken place. Appleyard was fined 5*s* and £1 2*s* 6*d* costs.

Affray with Bailiffs, Barnsley, 1884

. . . Marshall's wife came up and scratched Mr White on the face twice, while Marshall severely kicked him about the legs.

During the last week of February 1884, Wright Marshall, miner and Janet Marshall, his wife, of Dodworth Road, Barnsley, were before Alderman Tyas (Mayor), J Kaye, Esquire, R C Wilmot, Esquire and C Harvey Esquire, at Barnsley West Riding Court House, charged with assaulting County Court Bailiff, George White. On the previous Saturday Mr White said he saw Wright Marshall in Dodworth Road and told him he had a warrant against him for debt; to which Marshall replied that he would neither 'pay nor go'. Marshall was at that time looking in the *Boy and Barrel* window. Marshall took hold of Mr White and he was very violent. Then Marshall's wife came up and scratched Mr White on the face twice, while Marshall severely kicked him about the legs. Mr White took hold of Marshall's neck and Marshall bit his hand. A large crowd gathered and assisted Marshall to escape from the bailiff. Mr White lost his hat in the affray. Marshall insisted that White and another bailiff who accompanied him were drunk and that White struck him over the eye with his handcuffs. George Vale, foreman porter at the Court House Station, said he saw Mr White and another bailiff chasing the defendant and after they had caught him a scuffle ensued; and they tried to handcuff him. Two women were beating the bailiffs with an umbrella, and one of them was thrown down by one of the women. The bailiffs were badly used by the women and the crowd. Mr Vale said the bailiffs were quite sober.

The other bailiff, named Walton, said Janet Marshall and another woman pulled him away several times, and he was thrown down twice. Police Constable Gaythorpe said he saw the bailiffs after the affray and they were perfectly sober. White was bleeding behind one ear. Police Constable Barr also said the bailiffs were sober. For the defence, Priscilla Wilson said she saw White strike Marshall over the eye with the handcuffs. Emily Melvoy said she saw the bailiffs ill-using Marshall shamefully. The Mayor said the County Court Bailiffs had a right to be protected in the exercise of their duty. The Bench did not believe a syllable of the defence, and the charge had been greatly aggravated by the allegation that the bailiffs were drunk. Marshall was fined £2 and costs or a month's imprisonment. His wife was discharged.

Ruffian Assaults Auctioneer, Shales Moor, February 1892

Robson began to make a nuisance of himself, following Mr Jubb into Queen Street, where he became persistently abusive.

On Saturday 13 February, Albert Robson, a street peddler, who lived in Love Lane, was brought before magistrates at the Town Hall, charged with assault. The court heard that on the previous evening, Robson was in Shales Moor, where he approached the auctioneer, Mr J H Jubb, and asked him to buy something. Mr Jubb declined to buy anything and Robson began to make a nuisance of himself, following Mr Jubb into Queen Street, where he became persistently abusive. When Mr Jubb reiterated that he did not wish to buy anything, Robson struck him a violent blow in the face, causing his nose to bleed. Robson was quickly taken in charge and removed to the lock up. He was given a fine of 10*s*, or the option of seven days' imprisonment.

The Attercliffe Concealment of Birth Case, June 1892
She used the knife for the purpose of severing the umbilical cord, when her hand slipped and accidentally cut the child.

On Tuesday 4 August 1892, a twenty-three-year-old Attercliffe dressmaker appeared at Leeds Assizes before Mr Justice Grantham, indicted for the wilful murder of her illegitimate female infant, at Attercliffe, on 15 June. Mr C Mellor and Mr Edmondson, instructed by Mr Albert Howe, conducted the case for the prosecution. Edna Ashby, the woman concerned, was defended by Mr T E Ellison, instructed by Mr Arthur Neal. Miss Ashby remained seated in the dock throughout the proceedings, and was seen to weep from time to time. She was described as being of a highly respectable family.

The court heard that the prisoner gave birth to an illegitimate child without either the knowledge of her parents or any members of her family, on 15 June. Four days later she confessed that the birth had occurred and gave up the key to a drawer in her bedroom. The drawer contained the body of a dead female baby, and it bore a large and deep wound in the neck, which had evidently caused its death. The authorities were informed and the dead child's mother was arrested and charged with wilful murder. A series of court appearances followed resulting in Edna Ashby been committed to take her trial at the assizes, where she found herself that day.

The first witness to be called was the prisoner's mother, Martha Ashby and she repeated the evidence she had given before Sheffield coroner Dossey Wightman, Esquire and the town's stipendiary magistrate Edward M E Welby, Esquire, in which she stated that her daughter had had a child two years ago, being seduced under a promise of marriage. This same man was the father of her second child. Mrs Ashby added that her daughter was always an affectionate mother towards her first child and she did not believe her capable of wilfully harming one of her offspring.

His Lordship: *Who is this man? What is his name? There is no reason why his name should not be mentioned.*

Mrs Ashby: *I have never seen him for the last two years and a half.*

His Lordship: *Cannot you tell me who and what he is?*

Mrs Ashby: *He is a moulder, and his name is Thomas Farnsworth.*

Mrs Ashby went on to say that Farnsworth had disappeared soon after the child had been born and he had now disappeared again. She said she was not aware that her daughter had been seeing Farnsworth again. About six weeks before the second child was born she had sent for the surgeon, Mr Fitzpatrick, to examine her daughter, as she was in a very poor state of health. He had expressed the opinion that Miss Ashby was pregnant, a fact she vehemently denied.

Evidence was also given by Robert Ashby, the prisoner's father, and Mrs Eleanor Whitenear, her married sister. Mrs Whitenear said that she went to see her sister and noticed that something was amiss with her. After some questioning Miss Ashby eventually broke down and admitted to her that she had given birth. She then handed her sister the key to the drawer in which she had concealed the dead child.

Mr Alex Kirkpatrick, surgeon, of Attercliffe, said he was sent for by Mr Ashby, on 19 June. When he had entered Edna Ashby's bedroom, he was handed the key to a drawer. When he opened the drawer, he found the body of a newly born infant. There was a large incised wound on the side of the neck, probably inflicted by the table knife (which was shown to him in court), and which undoubtedly was the cause of death. The girl told him she was unattended when the child was born. She used the knife for the purpose of severing the umbilical cord, when her hand slipped and accidentally cut the child. Mr Kirkpatrick added that the position of the wound was consistent with such an accidental occurrence.

Mr H F N Scott, surgeon, of Attercliffe, said he made a post-mortem examination of the child's body, but was unable to say positively that the child had had a separate existence. It was a full-term child, and all its organs were healthy. It had breathed.

His Lordship, in his summing up, informed the jury that the law now enabled them to bring in a verdict of concealment of birth, when they were not satisfied that a person charged with causing the death of her child was guilty of wilful murder. Formerly there was no option but to acquit a prisoner in such a case. His Lordship said:

> *Before bringing in a verdict of guilty it is necessary to be satisfied that the child had had a separate existence, because if it was not fully born when the death was caused, the offence did not amount to murder, even if it were intentionally done. You are at liberty to find the prisoner not guilty on two grounds: firstly that separate existence had not been proved; and secondly, that the wound had been accidentally inflicted. That would leave behind the still serious crime of concealment of birth. In the meaning of the law the mere hiding of the body after birth amounted to concealment, and in coming to a decision on this point, you must not be influenced by sympathy with the young woman and consideration for her unhappy position, or indignation against the man who betrayed her.*

After retiring for fifteen minutes, the jury returned with their verdict. They found Edna Ashby not guilty of wilful murder, but that she was guilty of concealment of birth. The foreman then added that the jury also recommended her to mercy.

Addressing the prisoner, His Lordship said:

> *If I had thought that you intended to take the life of your child I should have certainly have passed a very severe sentence. But the evidence justifies me in coming to the conclusion that you had no such intention. The way in which you had treated your other child also justified one in coming to that conclusion. I think your offence is all summed up in the word 'concealment'. My sentence is that you be imprisoned for two calendar months, with such labour as you are able to perform.*

Edna Ashby was then taken down to commence her sentence.

Murderous Assault on a Lady During a Burglary, Hillsborough, July 1892

... dealt Mrs Thursfield a hefty blow on the forehead, knocking her unconscious.

Mr William Thursfield, manager of the Malin Bridge Works of Messrs Ward & Payne, lived at 78 Hunter Road, Hillsborough. On Saturday 23 July 1892, Mr Thursfield and his wife and daughter left their house at about 7.00 pm, Mr Thursfield having first secured the windows and doors in his usual fashion. Mrs Thursfield was the first to return home, arriving at the house at 10.30 pm. She noticed that a drawing room window at the front of the house was open. She went over and stood by the open window, where she heard someone moving about in the rooms. Alarmed that a burglary was being perpetrated, she immediately called out for assistance, hoping to secure the help of neighbours and passers by, but before help could arrive, just as Mrs Thursfield went past the front door of her home, it was immediately opened by the burglar who attempted to pass by her. She tried to prevent him doing so and a struggle ensued. Clearly in fear of being captured, the man drew an iron jemmy from his pocket and dealt Mrs Thursfield a hefty blow on the forehead, knocking her unconscious. As she fell to the ground bleeding profusely, the man made his escape into the dark night.

The Thursfields' next door neighbour, Mr William Wild, had heard Mrs Thursfield's cries for help and had speedily rushed to the front of the house. Unfortunately, he was not in time to prevent the burglar's escape but he was able to go quickly to his neighbour's assistance. Other neighbours soon arrived and medical assistance was sent for. Mrs Thursfield had received a severe head wound and lost a great quantity of blood. It was necessary to stitch the wound and it was only through her receiving speedy medical attention that loss of life was prevented. Police arrived and it soon became clear that the burglar had only just affected entry prior to Mrs Thursfield's return home, as nothing had been stolen, although two sacks, presumably ready to receive the felon's booty, had been left behind. The drawing-room window had been forced in such a manner that it was apparent that the burglar was not unfamiliar with that kind of work.

The incident gave local residents an opportunity to voice their views and vent their anger at the Lighting Committee, regarding a matter that had proved a bone of contention for some time, since during summer months they were being deprived of street lighting. Hunter Road was situated within an area known as the Land Society, which although the district had gas lamps and the residents paid lighting rates, they only had the advantage of street lighting at certain times of year. It was pointed out that the man who had perpetrated the burglary and murderous assault must have made his escape as several people were hurrying to the spot.

The lack of street lighting had clearly aided him in to escape into the dark without fear of being recognised or even noticed.

Assaulting a Railway Passenger, Mexborough, 1898

Fred Birkinshaw, plasterer, of Barnsley, said he saw Bowler strike Mr Speight as he stood in the doorway.

Barnsley Labourer Henry Bowler junior was summoned to Doncaster West Riding Court, on Saturday 30 April 1898, for wilfully interfering with the comfort of a passenger on the Great Central Railway at Mexborough, on 2 April.

Zachariah Speight, miner, of Barnsley, stated that on 2 April he was at Mexborough Station when the 8.10 pm train from Doncaster came in. He opened the carriage door and was about to board the train, when Bowler, who was inside the carriage, struck him in the face and pulled the door to. The blow caused an injury to Mr Speight's face and his mouth was bleeding. The Station Master, after enquiring into the matter had the defendant's name taken. Fred Birkinshaw, plasterer, of Barnsley, said he saw Bowler strike Mr Speight as he stood in the doorway. Robert Wild, Inspector at Mexborough Station, said he was told a fight was going on in one of the carriages, and on going there found Mr Speight with his mouth bleeding. Mr Speight then pointed out Bowler as being responsible for having knocked him out of the carriage, and when he was asked for his name and address by Inspector Wild, Bowler said he was Tom Jennings, of 5 Albion Street, Barnsley. There was some offensive and unpleasant language uttered by Bowler according to witnesses but Bowler tried to turn the tables by stating that Mr Speight had used offensive language in an attempt to gain entry to the carriage. There were already sixteen people in the carriage, according to Bowler, and subsequent evidence showed that Bowler's assertions of Mr Speight's bad language was not without foundation.

Witness Patrick Feeley said he was in the carriage, where there were sixteen or seventeen people. Bowler was standing with his back to the window. Mr Feeley saw the carriage door open, and Bowler was shoved across the carriage as a result of Mr Speight trying to get in. Bowler turned round and Zachariah Speight said he would get into the carriage. Bowler sat down and several others stood up, so Bowler could do nothing until a railway official came. The official asked, 'Who has done it?' and took a name. Mr Speight used a lot of fearful language after he had been injured which caused a woman passenger to leave the carriage. The Station Master was suspicious that Bowler had given a false name and address, so the police were called and Bowler was taken in charge. The Bench, having considered the evidence, fined Bowler 20s including costs.

CHAPTER 2

An Assortment of Edwardian and Early George V Misdemeanors

Goldthorpe Street Fighters Fined, 1900

There was a crowd of about 200 watching the fight . . .

Edward Garroghty and Frank McGowan were summoned to appear at Doncaster West Riding Court, in July 1900. G B C Yarborough, Esquire, was chairman of the Bench. The Bench were told that the two men were summoned for having obstructed the highway on Sunday evening, 8 July, when they were fighting opposite the club at Goldthorpe. There was a crowd of about 200

Doncaster Road, Goldthorpe c.1900, close to the spot where a crowd of 200 gathered to watch Edward Garroghty and Frank McGowan fight. Walkers Newsagents

Doncaster Road, Goldthorpe.

watching the fight, which caused the obstruction, when two cyclists drove up and were unable to pass. Mrs Ada Anderson gave corroborative evidence and both men were fined 5s and ordered to pay costs of 10s.

Illegal Betting in a Hoyland Garden, 1904
Witnesses were called who made bets in the greenhouse on Saturday.

By today's standards, a seemingly insignificant case made it onto the pages of a national newspaper, in 1904, such was the interest in illegal off-course betting at that time. On 1 September *The Times* reported on a case heard at Barnsley Court House, the previous day. Herbert Lindley, a bookmaker, of Hoyland, was charged with using his garden for betting purposes on certain days during the previous week. On Wednesday and Saturday the police said that 216 men were seen to go to Lindley's garden. Witnesses were called who made bets in the greenhouse on Saturday. The house and garden were raided, and in one book seized there were 600 entries relating to horses running that week, and to bets varying from £5 to 6d. A second book detailing 89 slips referred to 257 bets for Saturday's race meetings, and a third book contained 2,500 entries for bets placed recently. Lindley was given fines totalling £50 (a subtsantial sum, worth over £2,800 today).

Lodgings on the 'Nod', Ecclesfield and Conisbrough, 1907
Squires burst into a fit of sobbing, and complained bitterly that they would not give him a chance at all.

At the second court of the West Riding Sessions at Sheffield, on Friday 4 January 1908, engine driver Thomas Squires, described as an old and strange-looking man, of no fixed abode, was brought up on four indictments of larceny and false pretence. Two of the offences had been committed at Ecclesfield, where he had obtained food and lodgings under false pretences on 5 September 1907, from Harriet Walker; and in October he obtained food and lodgings from Annie Gabbitas, of Conisbrough, and on the 25th of that month he stole a watch and chain, the property of Patrick Fitzgerald, also at Conisbrough. Squires caused quite a stir in the courtroom by his strange behaviour. He acted in an hysterical manner following his admission to the offences he had been charged with, and appeared not to understand a word of what was being said to him. He continually protested to the court officials that if they were Christian people they would let him off, and finished off with a tirade of abuse, ending by exclaiming that all who told lies ought to drop dead. Having uttered these words Squires burst into a fit of sobbing, and complained bitterly that they would not give him a chance at all. It was necessary to remove him from the courtroom before the case was concluded. Sentence was passed in the prisoner's absence. Despite having denied any previous convictions just moments before in the courtroom, it was revealed that Squires had been in and out of prison since 1869. He was sentenced to a term of three years' imprisonment.

Assault at West Melton, 1909
Kerry struck the landlord a violent blow over the eye …

On Monday 3 January 1910, at Rotherham West Riding Court, miner Martin Kerry, of Bolton-upon-Dearne, was charged with assaulting Sam Cooper, licensee of the *Queens Hotel*, West Melton, on 11 December 1909; and, he was further charged with being disorderly and refusing to quit the hotel. In pleading guilty to each offence, he emphasised that he had great provocation to assault the landlord.

Appearing for the prosecution, Mr W M Gichard said that at nine o'clock on the night of 11 December, Kerry went into the hotel and asked for a glass of beer. He was in a sober condition and he was duly given the drink. Shortly afterwards Kerry began arguing with another customer and, after he became quarrelsome, the landlord ordered him to leave the premises, to which request, Kerry refused to oblige. After a little more trouble Kerry drank the remainder of his beer and walked out. He returned after a few minutes and went into another room. Fearing there might be trouble, the landlord asked him several times to leave the premises, but instead of complying with the request, Kerry struck the land-lord a violent blow over the eye, and a second one over the mouth, cutting his lip. At this point Mr Gichard pointed out that Kerry did not appear in court a fortnight before, as originally summoned, and it became necessary to issue a warrant for his arrest.

The landlord, Sam Cooper, and his son, James Cooper, gave evidence in support. Kerry said that when he was ordered out of the *Queens Hotel* he told the landlord he would finish drinking his beer before he went. He was going to do so, but the landlord took hold of him by the throat, which resulted in it being necessary to defend himself and Kerry contended that he had only struck out in self-defence. The Bench, which comprised E W Hodgkinson, Esquire and Dr J B Lyth, consulted for a few moments before giving Kerry a fine of 5*s* and costs or seven days, for refusing to quit, and for the assault 10*s* and costs or fourteen days.

Thefts at New Conisbrough, 1910

They were coming home with their husband's beer one night, and Annie asked her to hold the bottles while she picked a quilt off the line.

On Tuesday 1 March, a respectably dressed married woman, Phoebe Beckett, appeared before Doncaster magistrates, charged with stealing a shovel. She was further charged along with Annie Beckett, also a married woman, of New Conisbrough, with stealing a bed quilt. The shovel, which was produced in court, was identified by its owner, Margaret Thomas, of 9 Thornhill Street, New Conisbrough, who said that on 17 January at four o'clock in the afternoon, the shovel was in her back yard. A nine o'clock that same day she went to use the shovel and it was missing. The article was worth 2*s*.

Police Constable Grimshaw recovered the shovel from Jane Wigglesworth on 18 February. It had been sold to her by Phoebe Beckett. He charged Mrs Beckett with stealing the shovel and on being charged she replied:

I was hard up at the time.

Mrs Jane Wigglesworth, of 49 Clifton Street, New Conisbrough, said Phoebe Beckett had brought the shovel to her house on 19 January and had sold it to her for 1*s*. Mrs Wigglesworth said Phoebe had told her it had been brought home by her little boy. In her own defence, Phoebe Beckett told the Bench the shovel had been brought home from school by her little boy, and she sold it to get it out of the way, as her husband was constantly thrashing the boy over it. After a few moments hesitation Phoebe elected to give her evidence on oath. She said:

If I was to swear I took the shovel I should be telling a lie.

She added that it was on 2 February that her son had brought the shovel home from school.

The defendant's husband in his evidence said that when he came in from the pit on 2 February, 'the missus' told him that the lad had brought the shovel home. He told her it would have to be shifted and about a week later it was sold on condition it could be had back if the owner turned up. Mr Beckett admitted to Police Superintendent Hickes that his wife had been up for an offence in Staffordshire, coal-picking, or something like that.

On the second charge, Annie Glover, of 73 Blyth Street, New Conisbrough, gave evidence to the fact that she was missing a quilt valued at 7s which was taken from her washing line on 14 January. Emma Glynn, of Clifton Street, New Conisbrough, said that Phoebe Beckett had come to her house on 14 January and said to her:

I have got a pink fringe quilt from a house in Blyth Street.

She said that her sister-in law, Annie, had given her 4s for it. On 9 February, Mrs Glynn visited Annie's house at 56 Clifton Street, and she saw the quilt on the bed upstairs. Phoebe was in the house, she said:

This is the quilt I took from Blyth Street.

Police Constable Grimshaw visited the defendants' houses on 12 February. He found the quilt on a bed in Annie Beckett's house. She said she had brought it from Staffordshire about nine months ago. Annie Glover afterwards identified the quilt as her property. In answer to the charge Annie said that Phoebe took it off the clothes line to sell it to her. They were together at the time. Phoebe made no reply to the charge. At this stage Annie pleaded guilty to taking the quilt and Phoebe said she was with her at the time of the theft. Phoebe said her sister-in-law was not very well off at the time. They were coming home with their husband's beer one night, and Annie asked her to hold the bottles while she picked a quilt off the line.

There were three previous convictions against Phoebe Bennett for stealing. The chairman said it was a question whether they should send her to prison or not, but in the end they had decided they would give her another chance. She was fined 40s on each charge, or two months' prison in default. Annie was also fined 40s with the option of a month's imprisonment.

Thurnscoe Sensation, January 1912

*I meant to do her in. I have had it in my mind some
time. I cannot rest anywhere.*

Charles Crookes, miner, of Thurnscoe was brought up at Doncaster West Riding Court on Tuesday 9 January 1912, charged with attempting to murder his wife.

Police Superintendent Hickes said Mr & Mrs Crookes lived at King Street, Thurnscoe. For several weeks there had been quarrels between them. Owing to a quarrel in November the previous year, the wife, Emma Crookes, had gone to live with her son-in-law, Arthur Allington, who also lived in King Street. She lived with him for about three weeks. Her husband had accused her of being unfaithful, and the subject of his wife's unfaithfulness was the cause of many quarrels. On Saturday 23 December Charles and Emma Crookes went to Goldthorpe together, where they visited some public houses. They returned home at 10.15 pm. Whilst they were at Golthorpe they met a strange woman, who accompanied them home. The woman said she could not find lodgings and had nowhere to go, and Mr and Mrs Crookes said she could stay with them. Charles Crookes was slightly the worse for drink. The Crookes' son, Charles, aged nineteen, went to bed at 12.45 am, and Emma Crookes went to sleep on the sofa. Sometime after, she woke up and found the strange woman and her husband together. An argument ensued and Charles Crookes seized his wife by the hair and pulled her about. From that time Emma Crookes' mind was a blank, until she found herself in a house across the street, being attended to by a doctor. The son had apparently heard his mother scream, and jumping out of bed, had gone downstairs. He saw his father dragging his mother about by the hair. His father ordered him away and he went upstairs and dressed himself. Only partly dressed, he came back downstairs, in time to see his father take up a table knife from the dining table and dash with it at his mother.

Charles Crookes junior rushed outside and found Police Constables Wair and Statham, who went to the house but so no one there but the 'strange woman'. The house was in some disorder and there were signs of a great struggle having taken place. It appears that after the assault Mrs Crookes went across the street to the house of her son-in-law. She was bleeding from many wounds and said simply:

See what he has done.

At 12.15 am, Charles Crookes was arrested in the street, and on the way to the police station, he said:

I meant to do her in. I have had it in my mind some time. I cannot rest anywhere.

Mrs Emma Crookes, in her evidence, said, that when she awoke she saw her husband with his arms around the woman's neck. She asked him what he was doing, and he immediately went up to her, took hold of her by the hair and dragged her about the room. During cross-examination Mrs Crookes denied having been unfaithful to her husband and said on the whole he had been good to her.

The son, Charles Crookes, said that after his father and mother and the strange woman came to the house, his father fetched a jug of beer and a quantity of beer was also drawn from a barrel in the cellar. When he went to bed all three had had a good deal of drink, the strange woman being the worst of the three. Some time after he had gone to bed he heard his mother screaming and, on going downstairs, his father told him to go away. His mother said:

Fetch the bobbie, Charlie.

Robert Londesborough, screen-hand, of Thurnscoe, said that early in November he prevented the prisoner from assaulting his wife. The prisoner threw a water bottle at her, but it did not hit her. On 18 November he went with the prisoner to a singing room at Goldthorpe, where they saw Emma Crookes sitting with two other women, and the prisoner asked her to go out. She took no notice of him. He ran up to kick her, but Mr Londesborough said that he had stopped him. Whilst the prisoner was living apart from his wife he seemed very much depressed and one morning said to Mr Londesborough:

I can't get it out of my mind. I shall do it for her – it will come off.

He said he would do both his wife and children, and Mr Londesborough said to him:

Don't think that. Get it out of your head.

Susannah Jones, a married woman, of Thurnscoe, said she was living apart from her husband and acted as housekeeper to Mr Crookes whilst he was parted from his wife. She spoke to the woman coming to the house and heard the prisoner turn her out.

Dr R Malcolm, who was called to see the injured woman, said he found about twenty wounds upon her head, chest, shoulders and hands. There was a deep wound behind the left ear about half an inch long; a deep wound on the angle of the jaw, on the right side and a wound two inches long at the back of the hand. She had wounds on both hands

Mr Allen for the defence made an urgent plea to the Bench to reduce the charge to assault. The prisoner was committed to take his trial at the Assizes. Bail was refused.

On Tuesday 12 March, forty-seven-year-old Charles Crookes was tried at Leeds Assizes, before Mr Justice Avory, charged with inflicting grievous bodily harm upon his wife, Emma, and also with attempting to murder her. The prisoner pleaded guilty to the first charge, and the charge to attempted murder was withdrawn.

Counsel for the prosecution said that the prisoner had been married for twenty-six years, and, as far as he knew, up to about six weeks before the events responsible for the charges occurred, had lived happily with his wife. At that time his wife left him for a period of about three weeks, but returned to him. On the day in question both had been drinking in a public house, when they met a stranger to both, whom they took home with them. They reached the prisoner's house about a quarter past ten, and started drinking together again. The accused's son went to bed, but somewhere about midnight he was awakened by the screams of his mother. He went downstairs and saw that his father had got hold of his mother by the hair of her head. The prisoner's wife had stated that she had gone to sleep on the sofa leaving the strange woman and her husband drinking together, and when she awoke she saw them embracing and kissing each other. When she protested, he rushed at her, and seized her by the hair, and attacked her. She remembered no more, but the son had said that he saw his father get a knife off the table and cut his mother with it. The doctor who subsequently attended the woman found twenty wounds on her, mostly about the head and neck, all apparently inflicted by a knife.

The prisoner was in tears as Mr Justice Avory addressed him:

You have forfeited the character you have enjoyed for so many years. But there are circumstances in the case which justify me in sustaining

from passing on you a sentence of penal servitude. In this case there seems to be some reason for your jealousy of your wife, and having regard to the condition of your drunkenness both you and she were in at the time, I think I am justified in passing upon you a sentence of only fifteen months' hard labour.

The prisoner appeared somewhat relieved and simply replied:

Thank you, my Lord.

Mexborough Labourer Assaults Helpless Woman, December 1912

... he then struck her on the left side of the chin, knocking a tooth out.

Labourer Robert Smith, of Mexborough, was summoned on two counts by Doncaster magistrates. In the first instance Smith was summonsed by Police Constable Whiteman, for using obscene language at Mexborough on 23 December 1912; and in the second, by Bertha Wainwright, for having assaulted her on the same date. Police Constable Whiteman said that on the day in question he was on duty in company with Police Constable Chiddy, when he heard the defendant using very obscene language. He said he had:

*... given the ****** cow some ****** fist.*

Mr F Allen, solicitor appeared for the complainant, Mrs Wainwright, who went into the witness box swathed in bandages, said that she lived at 30 Market Street, Mexborough, and was the wife of boat hauler, John William Wainwright. On 23 December the defendant came into her house at 1.30 pm and assaulted her. Mrs Wainwright had just returned home from Mrs Bisby's, where she had been washing, and the defendant used abusive language to her. Mrs Wainwright ordered Smith out of the house and told him she would fetch a policeman if he didn't go. Smith refused to leave and struck Mrs Wainwright in the eye. She tried to get up by the table, and he then struck her on the left side of the chin, knocking a tooth out. He then punched her with his foot. He kicked her on her thigh violently, and she could not get up. A woman came and got him out of the house, whereupon he said:

*Let me go back and kick the ****** to death.*

Lily Benton, aged eleven, residing at Pitt Street, Mexborough, said she was at Mrs Wainwright's house and she saw Smith assault Mrs Wainwright. The little girl said she ran out of the house to find a policeman. Mrs Jane Bisby of Oxford House, Mexborough, said she saw Mrs Wainwright shortly after she had left Oxford House, and she was in a state. Smith was fined 2s 6d for using bad language and was sent to prison for fourteen days for the assault.

Rawmarsh Farmer Drunk in Charge of a Horse and Trap, 1913

I want to fight Lloyd George.

On Wednesday 1 January 1913, at 8.15 pm, Police Constable Rodgers was on duty in Main Street, Mexborough, in company with Police Constable Olive, when he saw a man in charge of a horse and dog cart. Police Constable Rodgers noticed that the cart was going from one side of the road to the other, so he brought the animal to a halt. Inside the cart was a man in a dazed and very drunken condition. When the constable spoke to the man about his reckless driving and asked him to get out of the dog cart, he refused to do so. When he was asked for his name and address, all the man could reply was 'Rawmarsh'. He started shouting:

I want to fight Lloyd George.

He was taken to Mexborough Police Station and locked up. The horse and cart were put up at the *Montagu Hotel*. The following day George Robinson, farmer, of Rawmarsh, was brought up before Doncaster magistrates, charged with being drunk in charge of a horse and trap. He pleaded guilty and said he was sorry for what had occurred. He was fined 2s 6d and costs.

Game Trespass, Hooton Pagnell, April 1913

Smith let his dog go when the hare got opposite, and the dog coursed the hare over several fields.

On Monday 14 April 1913, two South Elmsall miners, Herbert Chapman and Tom Smith, were charged at Doncaster, with trespassing for game on 2 April 1913. Prosecuting, Mr J Baddiley said that at 6.30 pm on the evening of 2 April, gamekeeper James Grass and his son, had concealed themselves in an old quarry when they saw the defendants coming along the road from Moorhouse to Hampole with a big black lurcher dog, which was eventually let loose after a hare. James Grass said that Chapman pointed to the hare, and Smith took his dog by the collar. Chapman went on to the lane, and drove a hare in the direction of Smith. Smith let his dog go when the hare got opposite, and the dog coursed the hare over several fields. Mr Grass caught the defendants up and charged them. They both gave their correct names and

addresses. Mr Grass saw the two men the next day and they said they were sorry. Chapman pleaded guilty and Smith pleaded not guilty. They were each fined 20s, including costs.

Indecent Assault, Goldthorpe, April 1913

Charles Neal ... on seeing Eliza Peddar, got hold of her leg, and then put his leg over hers.

On 5 April 1918 Eliza Peddar went to the *Horse and Groom Hotel* at Goldthorpe, where she seated herself on a ginger beer box outside. Pit worker Charles Neal came out of the public house and on seeing Eliza Peddar, got hold of her leg, and then put his leg over hers. She told him he ought to be ashamed of himself, whereupon he put his arm behind her back and tried to pull the box from underneath her. Mrs Peddar once again remonstrated with Neal about his behaviour, and he struck her and gave her a black eye. When Neal was brought up before Doncaster magistrates Mrs Annie Carney gave evidence. She said Neal made use of the most filthy expressions. Christopher Peddar, husband of the complainant, also gave evidence. Neal denied the assault, and said he was talking to a farm labourer and his wife. He denied having acted indecently towards Mrs Peddar and said he never made use of bad language. Ada Travis said that when Mrs Peddar got up to speak to another woman the defendant moved the box, and persisted in doing so. In fining Neal 40s and costs, the Chairman told Neal that if he came before the Bench for a similar offence again he would be more severely dealt with.

Barnsley Burglar Gaoled, 1916
I did it just for devilment; not because I wanted anything.

A twenty-five-year-old, one-handed miner, of John Edward Street, Barnsley, was brought before magistrates at Barnsley Borough Court on Thursday 1 March 1916, charged with burglary, breaking and entry, and theft.

The Bench were told that on 16 January, John Edward Street burgled the *Honeywell Inn*, and stole money and articles to the value of £3 6s 4d, the property of Benjamin Linsley and on the same day he stole a bicycle valued at £4 10s, the property of a mechanic, Frank Jackson. On 20 February Street broke and entered 18 The Arcade, occupied by J J Wilkins & Son, accountants, and stole money and articles valued at £10. Bertram James Wilkins was working at the office that day, which was Sunday. In the afternoon he returned to the office for a second time, when he found a cupboard door upstairs partly open. He tried to close this, but could not, and on looking behind the door he saw Steel, who immediately took some money from his pocket and placed it on the table. The police were sent for, and Police Constable Field searched Street and took him away.

Street had gained entry to the accountancy offices by breaking a pane of glass in the ground floor window at the back of the office, pushing back the catch, and taking out a screw. A roll-top desk downstairs had been forced open and ransacked. In addition to their being £7 4s 0d in Street's possession, were two fountain pens, a tape measure, and other articles totalling £10 in value.

Benjamin Linsley described the discovery of the theft at the *Honeywell Inn*, and told the Bench that in addition to stealing money and articles, Street had also stolen his Sunday dinner, as well. The stolen articles included cigars, cigarettes, a 16-ounce bottle of Oxo, two rabbits, a piece of pork, roller towels, glass cloths, forks, knives, spoons and a quart of whiskey.

With regard to the break in at the arcade, Police Constable Field said, when cautioned, that Street had replied:

I did it just for devilment; not because I wanted anything. I did not know there was any money there.

To the charge of breaking in to the *Honeywell Inn*, Street replied:

That is right.

Concerning the theft of the bicycle, Street admitted taking it from the back of the public hall. He asked the Bench to deal leniently with him, as this was the first time he had been in anything like this. He had a wife and child. When the Bench decided to commit him for trial, Street asked if he could have bail. He was told he could have bail – himself in £50 and two sureties of £25 each.

At the West Riding Spring Quarter Sessions Chairman of the Bench, William Sheepshanks, Esquire, was prompted to remark that it was extraordinary that a man with no previous convictions against him should be charged with all these offences. He had worked at various collieries in the Barnsley area during the last four years and when he was in full-time work earned as much as £2 7s 7d per week. Street said he was very sorry for what he had done and he would take care that he would do nothing of the kind again. His conduct had resulted in the loss of his home, and he had a wife and child who now had nowhere to go. He was sentenced to six months' imprisonment with hard labour, and ordered on his release to be placed under police supervision for a further six months.

Mexborough Suicide, January 1919

... death was due to poisoning by a strong corrosive acid, probably hydrofluoric acid, which he suspected the gutta-percha bottle contained.

Coroner Frank Allen, Esquire, held an inquest on Friday 24 January 1919 at the *Mason's Arms*, Doncaster Road, Mexborough, on the body of sixty-seven-year-old bricklayer, Albert Shaw, of 41 Hirstgate, Mexborough, who died on 22 January.

Henry Shaw, locomotive fireman, also of Hirstgate, son of the deceased, and living next door to his parents, said on Wednesday morning at four o'clock, he called at his father's house. His father was downstairs and he said he had been up all night with his mother. Henry Shaw had just finished working on the night shift, so he went home and after having his breakfast, he fell asleep by the fireside. His wife awoke him by calling downstairs that his mother was knocking on the wall. He went to his father's house, and saw his father standing against the kitchen table, with one hand on the table, while the other was drawing the back of a bread knife across his throat. Henry Shaw took the knife from his father, who was dazed and did not speak. He put his father in a chair and tried to give him water but his mouth was shut and his teeth were tightly clenched. The son then moved his father to the couch, where he died almost immediately. He was frothing at the mouth. Afterwards an old gutta-percha bottle was found on the sink, which according to the deceased man's wife had been in the house for thirty years. The deceased man had been depressed about his wife's illness and his own poor state of health for some time.

Dr J J Huey said he was sent for on Wednesday morning at 6.50 am, and found Albert Shaw was already dead. He made a post-mortem examination on Thursday, and in his opinion death was due to poisoning by a strong corrosive acid, probably hydrofluoric acid, which he suspected the gutta-percha (a rubbery substance, similar to plastic) bottle contained. The coroner said he was bound to come to the conclusion that the deceased took his own life and was probably not responsible for the action.

Grimethorpe Infested With Bookmakers, May 1919

You can search me. I have got nothing on me.

Making an appearance at Barnsley West Riding Court, on Friday 30 May 1919, was miner Arthur Richardson, of Grimethorpe, who denied a charge of street betting. Police Constable Pantry said he was concealed along with Sergeant Lamb and Constable Elliott on 13 May. They saw Arthur Richardson take up his stand at the corner of Hastings Street, about forty yards away, and in the course of half an hour, ten men handed him money and slips of paper.

A while later Richardson looked into the officer's hiding place, and on seeing them, ran home, fastening the door behind him. The police officers knocked on Richardson's door and after a few moments, he opened it. Richardson then said to the officers:

You can search me. I have got nothing on me.

When told he would be reported, he said:

It will be a lesson to me. I have only been demobilised a fortnight.

An early twentieth-century view of High Street, Grimethorpe. Old Barnsley

Sergeant Lamb said that Grimethorpe was infested with book-makers, there being about a dozen in the village.

Police Constable Elliott, who also gave evidence, was asked by Superintendent McDonald if he agreed that bookmaking was doing great harm at Grimethorpe, to which the constable said that it was a perfect nuisance. Complaints were made daily of women and children being mixed up with betting. Richardson admitted touting for another man but denied having taken any money for bets. He was given a fine of £10.

On the following Wednesday, 4 June, Samuel Thomas, book-maker of Grimethorpe, pleaded guilty to street betting in that place. Police Superintendent McDonald said that Sergeant Lamb and Police Constable Elliott watched Thomas from 10.50 am to 12.30 pm, and saw him take money and slips of paper from nine-teen men. The officers arrested Thomas and searched him, and they found as a result of his morning's work he cleared £3 profit. Thomas was the fourth bookmaker to be brought to that Court from Grimethorpe, so far that year. Three new ones had started bookmaking there during the previous week, where soldiers came and went with £10 to £20 gratuity money. The bookmakers openly stated they were after this gratuity money. Superintendent

McDonald asked for the full penalty as that was the only way to stop this evil. Thomas, who was unable to work, pleaded for leniency but as he had a previous conviction the Bench fined him a substantial £20 (over £424 today).

Smart Fine for Unprovoked Darton Assault, 1919

... *Pell knocked him off a stool and struck him on the head twice with a glass.*

Described as being middle-aged, Darton miner Enoch Pell, pleaded guilty, when he appeared at Barnsley West Riding Court, on Monday 5 January 1920, charged with assaulting Wilfred Moore, of Bridge Street, Darton.

Prosecuting, Mr Rideal said Pell was arguing with another man on Boxing Day, at the *Darton Hotel*, and upon Mr Moore making some remark, Pell knocked him off a stool and struck him on the head twice with a glass. This had caused three wounds, which had necessitated four stitches and Mr Moore had been off work since the incident.

For the defence, Mr Pratt said, that at the time the incident occurred, Pell was in an excited state and under the influence of drink, and struck the blow in the heat of the moment. Chairman of the Bench, W Dutson, Esquire, pointed out that this was Pell's *nineteenth* appearance in court, and if drink led him to do such things the Bench recommended him to leave it alone. Pell was fined £5 and costs, 50s of the fine to go to Wilfred Moore by way of compensation, or the option of two months' imprisonment.

CHAPTER 3

Foul Deeds From the 1920s to the 1950s

Thief and Failed Suicide, Wath-upon-Dearne, 1922

Fetch Mrs Secker and my husband. I have been trying to poison myself.

Twenty-nine-year-old Mrs Mary Ann Parkes, of 23 Littlemore Road, Wath-upon-Dearne, stood in the dock before E Rose, Esquire and W H Hallatt, Esquire, at Rotherham West Riding Police Court, on Tuesday 18 July 1922, charged with having attempted to commit suicide, and with having stolen a quantity of clothing, valued at £2.

Alice Elizabeth Needham said she lived with her husband at Wath, and the defendant and her husband had lodged with them since September On 4 July Mrs Needham was in the kitchen, when the defendant rushed in from out of the front room and kissed her on the cheek, then exclaimed, 'Oh, missus!' She then dropped on the couch and asked for a drink of water. Mrs Needham gave her a drink, and Mrs Parkes then said:

Fetch Mrs Secker and my husband. I have been trying to poison myself.

The police and a doctor were called in. Police Constable Sagar said that at 9.30 am on 4 July he went to the house of the defendant and saw her lying on the couch. He gave her something to make her vomit, and she afterwards appeared a little better. He asked her what she had taken, and she replied 'Parazone'. He found an unfinished note in her handwriting, addressed to her husband and the landlady.

With regard to the second charge, Mrs Alice Needham, said at 7.30 pm on 3 July, on looking through some drawers, she missed a white bed-rug and a quantity of clothing. She wrote a list of missing articles on a piece of paper, and asked the defendant if she had had them. She replied:

I have had them, but I was forced to take them. I will fetch them tomorrow. They are at a pawnbroker's at Mexborough. Don't tell my husband. Will you take my little girl, aged three, because I am going to do away with myself.

Mrs Needham said she would not tell her husband but she would not take the little girl, and Mrs Parkes said she would not do away with herself. Fourteen-year-old Mary Elizabeth Secker, said she had pawned articles of clothing at Mexborough for the defendant.

Mrs Parkes said she had been driven to it and they were:

... throwing it in her face now that she did not take enough stuff to kill her. The landlady gave me the clothes to pawn for her.

Mrs Needham denied that she had ever given Mrs Parkes any items to pawn for her.

Mary Ann Parkes was bound over in the sum of £5 to be of good behaviour for two years, and was placed under the supervision of the probation officer. She was also ordered to pay 9s to the pawn-broker and 15s costs.

Armed Night Poaching, Wombwell Wood, 1923
Halt ... don't come any further or I will fire.

In the early hours of Sunday 28 October 1923, three Womb-well miners: Harry Wigglesworth, aged twenty-four, of 56 Blythe Road, Wombwell, Edward Dyson, aged twenty-four, of Station Road, Wombwell and Jospeh Dyson, aged twenty-eight, of Edward Street, Wombwell, were apprehended by four game-keepers on Captain Wentworth's land in Wombwell Wood. On Friday 2 November, the four men appeared before magistrates at Barnsley West Riding Court, on a charge of night poaching. Joseph Dyson was also charged with shooting with intent, and Edward Dyson with inflicting grievous bodily harm.

Mr Rideal prosecuted and said that in the early hours of the morning in question, four keepers were in Ringley Carr Wood at Wombwell. About 3.30 am, they heard two shots fired at a dist-ance of about fifty yards away. The keepers were standing by a wall. Shortly after the shots were fired Harry Wigglesworth and Joseph Dyson came over the wall, and Edward Dyson came up to the wall. Richard Rogers, one of the keepers, said:

When I got to the wall I went for Wigglesworth, who struck at me with an ash sapling and then ran in the direction of another watcher, Manley, who seized him. I saw Joseph Dyson running away, with a gun, and next I saw my fellow keeper, Ratcliffe, lying in a semiconscious condition, with blood on his face. At the same time I saw Edward Dyson running away towards the road. I returned to Manley and secured Wigglesworth and took him to my home. On the way I heard another shot fired. I later identified both the Dysons at a parade at the Court House.

Gamewatcher, Samuel Manley, said that he had closed with Wigglesworth after he had been struck by him. Another part-time watcher, plate-layer, George Taylor, said that he made for Joseph Dyson, who was then ten yards away. Dyson produced a gun concealed about his person, and while Dyson made his escape, Taylor followed him. As Taylor was in pursuit, Dyson turned round and said:

Halt . . . don't come any further or I will fire.

Dyson started to run again, with Taylor hot on his heels. Then from a distance of about thirty yards, Dyson turned round, put the gun to his shoulder, took a deliberate aim, and fired, but the shot missed.

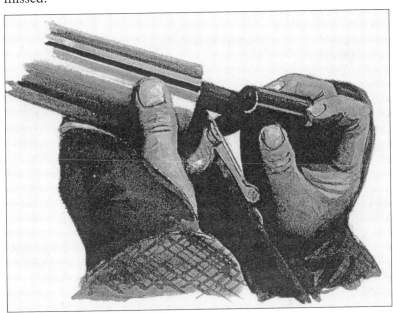

Thomas Ratcliffe, who appeared in court with his head bandaged, said that as he went to seize Edward Dyson, Dyson threw a stone at him which struck him on the head:

I knew no more after that,

he said.

Dr Barclay Wiggins, of Thistle House, Hoyland, said that Ratcliffe had a wound an inch long in the middle of the forehead, which penetrated to the bone. His clothing was saturated with blood.

Police Constable Laws said that in Wigglesworth's pockets were three newly killed pheasants. The Dysons, when asked to account for their movements in question, said they were in bed. No gun had been found. The Bench committed all four to take their trial at the Assizes. The men reserved their defence and all were allowed bail.

The case came up at Leeds Assizes before Mr Justice McCardie, on Tuesday 11 December. Mr F J O Coddington prosecuted and Mr W P Donald defended.

In the witness box, Edward Dyson stated that he went home about ten o'clock and went to bed. He got up at nine o'clock the following morning, and was not out of bed during the night. Joseph Dyson admitted trespassing in the pursuit of game but denied that he had fired at one of the keepers. He said when they ran after him he had fired in the air to frighten them. Dyson went on to say that his brother Edward was not with him that night but declined to name the third man.

Edward Dyson was found not guilty on all charges. Joseph Dyson and Harry Wigglesworth were found guilty of night poaching. Joseph Dyson was found not guilty of shooting with intent. Edward Dyson was discharged but Harry Wigglesworth and Joseph Dyson were each sentenced to seven months' imprisonment with hard labour.

Darton Main Deputy's Offence, 1925

... Hartley failed to load the material in a specially marked tub ...

Edward Hartley, a deputy, employed at Darton Main Colliery, appeared before magistrates at Barnsley's West Riding Court on

Wednesday 18 February 1925, charged with a breach of regulations in connection with the firing of a shot. The Bench heard that after a shot had been fired Hartley failed to load the material in a specially marked tub, and the full charge and detonator were found the next day by men picking dirt from the tubs. Prosecuting, Mr A S Smith, said:

> *... There might have been a terrible explosion and loss of life ...*

Hartley was fined 40*s* and costs.

Great Houghton Hawker Gaoled, 1926

... he called on a large number of householders at Goldthorpe, with a plea for money, saying he was on an errand of mercy ...

Sixty-two-year-old Hawker, Frederick R Oldfield, of Great Houghton, appeared before Doncaster West Riding magistrates on Tuesday 8 February 1926, charged with obtaining money by false pretences. Oldfield pleaded guilty. The Bench heard that he had obtained 2*s* from Walter Spencer; 2*s* 6*d* from George Morley; and 2*s* 6*d* from Edwin H West, as well as other smaller sums of money.

Police Superintendent Minty, outlining the facts of the case, said that on 31 January, Oldfield was out at work and on that day and on subsequent dates he called on a large number of householders at Goldthorpe, with a plea for money, saying he was on an errand of mercy, which he explained was for the benefit of out-of-work miners who had been thrown on the dole, and were destitute. In this way he obtained several small sums of money which he spent on drink. There were six charges of obtaining money by false pretences and thirteen of attempting to do so.

Superintendent Minty said he had had a chance before. On 5 September 1925 at Doncaster Borough Sessions he was convicted for obtaining £2 15*s* by false pretences and was sentenced to hard labour. Oldfield said he was very sorry, he was getting on in years. The Chairman, J Brocklesby, Esquire, told Oldfield:

> *Your conduct has been very obnoxious. You have spent the money on drink. Can you think of anything more contemptible? I cannot.*

Oldfield was sentenced to three months' imprisonment with hard labour.

Hooliganism at Mexborough, 1927

It is an outrageous case. You three men have behaved like hooligans.

William Wright senior, William Wright junior and Tom Grey, all miners, of Mexborough, were charged before Doncaster magistrates, on Tuesday 12 April 1927, with having assaulted Joseph Ryder, miner, also of Mexborough. G B Shiffner, Esquire was Chairman of the Bench.

Ryder said that at 10.45 pm, on 18 March, he got off a Blue Bus at West Street, Mexborough, and walked along Main Street to his house, with a pipe in his mouth and his hands in his pockets. Grey went up to him and hit him in the face. The elder Wright followed Grey and hit him in the mouth, knocking his pipe out, and the younger Wright hit him in the eye. Ryder, in pulling his hand from his pocket, pulled some money out, which dropped on the floor.

Ethel Jenkinson said she saw Ryder hit three times by each defendant. She protested and was told to get away. Mrs Wright, who was also present, shouted:

> *He is getting all he deserves. He is only a ***** blackleg, a scab, and a gaffer's man.*

A bus had to stop to let Joseph Ryder get up off the ground. Mrs Jenkinson said that on 20 March, Grey and Wright junior visited her and asked if she was appearing as a witness. She said she did not know, and Wright told her if she did not appear he had a bank book, and they had some pigs. The visit was obviously intended to persuade Mrs Jenkinson not to appear by promises of money and home fed pork. She simply told the defendants they should not have hit Ryder.

Joseph Stead, of Mexborough, said that at about 10.45 pm he was walking down High Street and saw Ryder on the floor. He also saw Grey kick Ryder. Joseph Greenwood, of Belmont Street, Mexborough, said at about 10.45 pm he was at the top of Belmont Street, when he saw Ryder walking towards him with his hands in his pockets. Grey and the two Wrights, with Mrs Wright, approached Ryder. Grey struck Ryder, who went down. He also saw the two Wrights strike Ryder, who fell on each occasion. He heard Wright junior when passing him say,

> *I kicked him.*

Wright junior then stooped and picked some mud up off the ground to cover some blood on the pathway.

Police Constable Aucock said he made enquiries and saw the three defendants. Grey said:

I only hit him once. The man insulted me. What would you have done?

Wright junior said:

I hit him.

Wright senior said:

We will show him what we can do.

Tom Grey said he commenced work at Cadeby Colliery on 1 March, but owing to illness he had to have several days off. On 18 March, Ryder, who was the headman in Grey's stall (workplace at the coalface), collected money for the stall. Grey saw Tyder in the pit yard and was offered a 1s as a day's wage, which Grey claimed for. Grey said he ought to have had about 13s. They arranged to meet when Ryder got off the bus at West Street that night. He met him as arranged, and was talking to him for about ten minutes. Ryder refused to pay, and struck him on the face and knocked him down.

William Wright senior said that Ryder struck Grey, but he did not hear any conversation. Grey then got up from the floor and struck Ryder. He lifted him from the floor and Ryder ran away. He did not strike Ryder. William Wright junior was the next witness. He said he had been with his parents to a whist drive at the British Legion. He denied taking part in the assault, and said he was never near Ryder.

The chairman said:

It is an outrageous case. You three men have behaved like hooligans.

Wright junior had six previous convictions, including one for assault on the police. Grey had two previous convictions for common assault, and Wright senior, three convictions. They were each sent to prison for two months, with hard labour.

Magistrates' Clerk Mr E W Pettifer said to Mrs Jenkinson:

The Bench would like to commend your action in coming forward. You protested at the time very courageously. The Bench commend you for your action, and accept your evidence as literally true.

Staincross Man's Rat Poison Suicide, 1933

... he had told her she would not see him alive again.

An inquest was held before Deputy Coroner S H B Gill at the Barnsley Municipal Institution, on Tuesday 25 July 1933, on an ex-soldier who saw war service when he was just seventeen years old. A sad catalogue of events was revealed concerning a painful story of domestic unhappiness, which led to thirty-six-year-old miner Richard Howarth, of 5 Hunningley Terrace, Staincross, taking rat poison.

Mary Howarth, who had separated from her husband on 26 April, now lived and worked in Rotherham. She said her husband, who worked at Woolley Colliery, enjoyed good health. The couple did not get on, although they had had five children together, who were living with their father up to the time of his death. Mrs Howarth said she last saw her husband on Monday 17 July when he went over to Rotherham and he had told her she would not see him alive again. He had attempted to take his own life previously, in December 1932, when he had tried to gas himself.

The deceased's father, Richard Howarth, also of 5 Hunningley Terrace, Staincross, said:

I served twenty-nine years in the West Riding Police Force and have been retired about fourteen years. My son joined the Army when he was 17½ years old and spent his eighteenth birthday in the firing line. He enlisted on Easter Monday 1915, and before that was a bright, cheerful lad. After leaving the army he was very strange. He would deliberately break an ornament and the next thing he would say he was sorry he had done it. He was gassed at the front in 1917 and there is no doubt his war service affected him. Really, he thought the world of his wife when he was alright. Suddenly, he would fly into a passion, and then, after his wife had left him, he would be crying for her back, praising her, and giving her all the credit anyone could.

Mr Howarth said that on his return from Rotherham the previous week, his son had said to him:

Well father, she's not coming back. I'm going to give the children away.

He also said that he was going to break the home up and 'do himself in'. He also asked to be buried in his mother's grave. Mr Howarth added:

I tried to pacify him but his mind did not seem at rest.

Mr Howarth said that his son ate good meals on the previous Tuesday but at about six o'clock in the evening he began complaining of stomach pains, which grew gradually worse. He asked for a doctor but denied having taken anything. He subsequently admitted to his father that he had taken rat poison. Mr Howarth said:

> *I have given my son every help I possibly could. I own the house and allowed them to live rent free. I always put his trouble down to going through the war when he was so young.*

Dr R Millar, of Darton, said he suspected poisoning when he first attended to Richard Howarth. It was only later that his patient admitted that he had taken rat poison. When asked by the coroner what sort of poison this was, the doctor replied:

> *Phosphorous poison.*

Dr Millar went on to say that he had made a post-mortem examination, and in his opinion the cause of death was phosphorous poisoning.

Police Constable Howard said that in the ambulance on the way to Barnsley Municipal Institution the deceased had said:

> *I have been to see my wife at Rotherham. I have nothing to live for. I bought a 7½d tin of rat poison. I took about half of it. I have thrown the tin in the plantation at the back of our house.*

The tin was found there the next day. Richard Howarth died on Sunday 23 July. The coroner returned a verdict of 'Suicide by taking rat poison during temporary insanity'.

Husband Gambled Money Given to Provide for Family, Burton Grange (Monk Bretton), 1939

He gambled the money he received, at Ardsley Wood and Kimberley by tossing.

The Mayor, Councillor H M Cassells, was presiding at the County Borough Police Court, at Barnsley, on Thursday 20 April 1939, when Clement Dobson, of 3 Friars Road, Burton Grange, was brought up before the Bench, summoned for neglecting his three children, in a manner likely to cause unnecessary suffering or injury to their health.

Mr J G E Rideal, prosecuting on behalf of the NSPCC, said the case first came under the notice of the Society in November 1936, and Dobson had been warned repeatedly. He was visited regularly by the Inspector up to December 1937, when the man was considered to be satisfactory. Recently, another complaint was received by the Inspector and when he visited the house there was hardly any food so he bought some. When his wife had complained of him neglecting them he had ill-treated her. Dobson visited Ardsley Wood or Kinsley, where there were gambling schools and lost the money received from the Unemployment Assistance Board. Neighbours had given his wife food for herself and children.

On April 8 Dobson left to draw his money and the children had about six potato chips each for their dinners. He arrived back home at 7.45 pm and said he had no money. On Good Friday, the following day, Mrs Dobson had to borrow money for food. Mr Rideal said had it not been for the neighbours giving the mother money, the children would have starved. Since the Inspector visited, Dobson took 6s out of his wife's purse, and he had taken 2s 6d previously for spending money. Dobson received money from the authorities to spend on his home and family but did not do so.

Hilda Dobson said her husband became unemployed three years ago. She had been short of money, but afraid to report the matter because he ill-treated her. He gambled the money he received, at Ardsley Wood and Kimberley by tossing. He owed £26 0s 6d for rent, and had it not been for his father and neighbours, who had given them money for food, they would have starved. He had ill-treated her day after day, and stood over her and threatened that if she went to court that morning and said if she said anything against him, he would stick a knife through her heart.

Mr Rideal asked,

Are you afraid of him?

Mrs Dobson replied,

I have always been afraid of him or I should have been here before.

Mrs Dobson said that on 6 April she gave her children about six potato chips each for dinner, about 11.30 am, and they had had nothing more when her husband returned without money, and were huddled together in a chair, fast asleep. The children were all very young. Peter was aged seven, Molly aged five and June aged three. Mrs Dobson said she kept the children up in case her husband came home with any food. Mrs Dobson, in reply to a comment made by her husband, said that he once bought the children boots out of his winnings, but denied that she had left the children unattended while she went to dances. She once went with Dobson's sister for half-an-hour, with her husband's permission, and he was in the house. When asked if she had not spent money on cosmetics, she replied:

I don't think I have had any powder on my face for two years.

Lewis Alexander Marshall, Unemployment Assistance Board Officer, said in consequence of Dobson's gambling, which he frankly admitted, they had to provide grant relief to Mrs Dobson on several occasions.

Inspector Rawlings of the NSPCC, bore out Mr Rideal's statement, then added:

I have repeatedly warned this man. He has got the gambling fever in his blood and does not care what happens. The man has no regard for his children at all; he only wants money in his pocket.

Dobson admitted he had gambled but asserted that he had used the money to good advantage when he had won, by buying shoes, clothing and food for his children. He realized he had been a fool but never had he returned the next day to gamble his winnings. Dobson then added:

There are not three healthier and more contented children on the estate than ours.

The Mayor, addressing the prisoner, said:

The Bench have seriously considered this case and it would appear that repeated warnings by the Inspector have been of no avail. You will be committed to prison for one month with hard labour.

Mother and Daughter Gaoled, Barnsley, 1947

... she later admitted having received from her mother ...

Housewife Sarah Jane Blessed, aged fifty-five, of 9 Boundary Street, Barnsley and her daughter, thirty-six-year-old widow Dora Dudley, of 12 Boundary Street, appeared at Barnsley Borough

Magistrates' Court on Monday 1 September 1947, charged with shoplifting and 'receiving' respectively. Police Superintendent Legg said the fact that Jane Blessed had gone out shoplifting on numerous occasions was clearly indicated by the number of articles stolen and the period in which the offences were committed. She was charged with stealing socks, soap, and parcel labels, valued at 4s 6d, from two Barnsley chainstores. Her daughter was charged with receiving from her a handbag and a pair of gloves, valued at £1 11s 6d and also a pair of children's shoes; and two pairs of socks valued at 10s 11d. In addition to those items, Blessed asked for several other cases of stealing clothing, cutlery, toiletry requisites and household goods, valued at £11 4s 11d, stolen from four Barnsley stores between 23 December 1946 and 20 August 1947, to be taken into consideration.

Superintendent Legg said that on 20 August at one particular chainstore, supervisor Kathleen Lowe, saw Blessed place several pairs of white socks inside her coat while an assistant's back was turned. Shortly afterwards Blessed left the store and the assistant manager followed her and stopped her in Market Street. On being confronted about the stolen goods, Blessed said:

I'm terribly sorry. I want to pay for them.

She then offered the assistant manager £1 which he refused to take. The police were informed and when arrested Blessed re-iterated that she wanted to pay for the goods. When asked why she had taken the socks, she replied:

For my grandchild.

On being searched a quantity of soap and some parcel labels were also found in her possession. On being informed of the charges against her mother Dudley denied having received any goods from her, at first maintaining several items she later admitted having received from her mother, had in fact been purchased by herself in Leeds. Concerning a handbag and some gloves, Dudley later admitted:

My mother gave the handbag and gloves to me last Christmas, and the shoes and socks a few weeks ago. I had an idea they were stolen and was trying to shield her.

Dora Dudley had three children under fourteen-years-old and a total income of £2 4s. per week. As to her previous record,

Superintendent Legg said in 1932 Dudley was bound over for six months for stealing ladies' clothing and twelve months for stealing a postal order. In 1941 she was bound over for twelve months for stealing and in August 1942 she was fined £5 for stealing a jumper suit; and in October 1942 bound over for twelve months for stealing a perambulator and other articles.

Chairman of the Bench, R J Soper, Esquire, said:

> *The Bench has no option but to deal with you in a manner you both deserve. You are liable to go to prison for twelve months and we cannot allow these cases to go unpunished in the interest of shopkeepers and the general public. Therefore, you, Jane Blessed, will go to prison for two months on each charge, the sentences to run concurrently; and you, Dora Dudley, will go to prison for two concurrent periods of one month.*

Heartless Husband Gaoled for Neglect, Swinton, 1952

I saw him brand his wife on the arm with a hot poker which he had taken from the fire.

A twenty-eight-year-old labourer, Rhuland Walford, of Toll Bar Road, Swinton, was sent to prison for six months by the Doncaster West Riding Magistrates, on Tuesday 27 May 1952, for neglecting his three children. He pleaded guilty to the charge.

The Bench were told that Walford had three young children, Rhuland, aged seven, David John, aged five, and Odette, aged sixteen months, living with their mother at Mexborough. Mr C Keeton, prosecuting for the NSPCC, said that Walford had kept his wife and family very short of money throughout their married life. His wife had obtained two separation orders in 1948 and 1950, and had started divorce proceedings which she had been persuaded to stop. Mr Keeton said:

> *She has had nothing whatever from him since March 7th this year, and since August she has drawn £72 from the National Assistance Board. His wife has had very little for a matter of six years in the way of money. Since Walford left the RAF in 1946 he has worked for a few weeks and then been absent from work.*

Inspector J Preston of the NSPCC, said:

> *This woman is definitely afraid of this man. Since the present proceedings were instituted Walford has never supported his wife, except*

for a very brief period at the beginning of the year. Since this summons was issued the wife has been afraid to go out of the house at night because her husband has told her that if he has to go to prison he will go for something proper and he intends to do her some injury. She is a remarkably clean woman and does her duties excellently.

Mr Keeton read out a statement made by Mrs Walford's neighbour, Mrs Muriel Skirrow, of 10 Foundry Lane, Mexborough, who had helped Mrs Walford on many occasions. In her statement Mrs Skirrow wrote:

On one occasion two years ago I saw him gag her and tie her up in a basket chair. I saw him brand his wife on the arm with a hot poker which he had taken from the fire. He had a razor blade tied between two pieces of wood and was going to cut her throat. On many occasions I have fed Mrs Walford and her children when she has been without food and in fact since the birth of Odette she has almost been maintained by me with food. After the baby was born and she was about one month old, he turned her out into the street at about 4.30 in the morning.

The prisoner said nothing as he was taken away from the courtroom to begin his sentence.

Doncaster Youth's Suicide at Conisbrough, 1952

When it was almost level he jumped as if he was jumping into a swimming bath.

A seventeen-year-old, former Doncaster Grammar School pupil, chose to end his life in a spectacular way, when on Tuesday 8 July 1952 at 5.30 pm, he threw himself in front of a train. 'B', of Hexthorpe, who was serving his articles with a Doncaster firm of auctioneers, leapt to his death on the main Doncaster to Sheffield line, about half a mile from Conisbrough Station, between Conisbrough and Doncaster.

A inquest was held on Friday 11 July at Conisbrough, before Doncaster District Coroner W H Carille.

The deceased's mother, said her son had been a nervous child, who had not enjoyed good health, then added:

He recently passed an examination in which he was one of the youngest entrants. He had been studying hard. He was the best lad anyone could meet both at work and at home and he has been my right hand. I gave him 5s a week pocket money and any overtime money he earned. Recently he had met a girl and at first they seemed to have hit it off. Later I told him it would only lead to trouble ... I last saw him at 12.50 pm on the day he died ...

Engine driver Charles Chappel, of Mexborough, said his engine was approaching a crossing near the Cliff sidings about half a mile from Conisbrough, when he saw a youth walk across the line in front of the train. The boy had ample time to get across the line and he stood watching as the engine approached:

When it was almost level he jumped as if he was jumping into a swimming bath.

Mr Chappel having pulled the train to a halt, dismounted from his cab and went to investigate. Having found the youth's body below the bogey wheels, there was nothing he could do except go on to Conisbrough and inform the station staff what had occurred.

The Station Master at Conisbrough, Mr Norman Mitchell, said he went up the track with two policeman and found the youth's dismembered body in the four foot way at the side of the track. One of the policemen, Sergeant Percy Johnson, said he found the 'B's' bicycle at the side of a footpath, about forty yards from the line on the Cadeby side of the track.

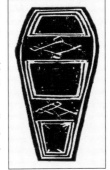

The coroner recorded a verdict that the young man 'committed suicide while the balance of his mind was disturbed'.

Mr Walter Bell, auctioneer and valuer, whose firm that dead boy was articled to described his deceased employee as being 'extremely intelligent and self possessed'.

Determined Denaby Suicide Dies in Canal, 1952

... during recent months had been somewhat deluded, having convinced himself that 'people were talking about him.'

On the night of 24 October 1952, sixty-seven-year-old 'V', of Denaby, disappeared from home. His housekeeper, Mrs Isabella

Hobson, and also his lodger, seventy-seven-year-old bricklayer's labourer, Will Coleman, conducted an extensive search for him in the pouring rain, before eventually reporting him missing to police. 'V's body was recovered from the canal near Denaby Low Lock the following Thursday.

An inquest was held on Saturday 1 September at Denaby, before the District Coroner, W H Carille, Esquire. The deceased's housekeeper, said 'V' had been in ill health for several years and during recent months had been somewhat deluded, having convinced himself that 'people were talking about him'. His wife went on to say that in September 1951, her husband underwent an operation at Rotherham, and in October had spent a fortnight in hospital at Balby. It was after his discharge from hospital that he began to suffer from these delusions.

Police Sergeant E Theaker said that on Thursday 30 October, having received a message from lock-keeper, Mr Arthur Wood, he had gone to the canal and shortly afterwards recovered the body of 'V' from the water.

Doncaster pathologist, Dr P N Waugh, said that he had conducted a post-mortem examination on the body. There were no marks of violence and death was due to asphyxia consistent with drowning.

Two pieces of rope were shown in evidence. These had been used to secure the deceased's hands and feet before he had plunged into the water. Mr Carille said:

> 'V' disappeared from home on the night of October 24th, and had obviously decided to end his life. He, being a good swimmer, in an effort to prevent him from saving himself 'V' had tied his hands and feet together.

The coroner recorded a verdict of 'suicide while the balance of his mind was disturbed'.

Double Life Led by Hoyland Boy Sunday School Teacher, 1953

I like boys to interest themselves in the Church but this boy is leading what might be termed a double life . . .

A fifteen-year-old Hoyland Sunday School teacher appeared with a fifteen-year-old friend from Wentworth in the dock at Rotherham Juvenile Court, charged with stealing. The boys were charged with stealing two lots of books and maps from a Rotherham shop, valued at £1 17s 2d. Both boys asked for two other offences of stealing and two at Barnsley to be taken into consideration.

A West Riding Child Care Officer, Miss Unwick, said the Hoyland boy was a Sunday School teacher, who had done very well since leaving an approved school. The other boy had not been in trouble before. Chairman of the Bench, W O Dent, Esquire, said:

> *We want this taking to the people who are permitting this lad to be a Sunday School teacher. I like boys to interest themselves in the Church, but this boy is leading what might be termed a double life.*

Councillor J H Dickinson, a member of the Bench, who raised the question of the boy's Sunday School teaching, said:

> *I think it's absolutely crazy.*

Mr Dent said:

> *I have never known religion dragged in the dirt so much as it has been here today. He goes to communion and then to the Wesleyans because he has some pals there.*

Both boys were each given the maximum fine possible, £10 and ordered to pay costs.

CHAPTER 4

Highway Robbery in Wentworth Park
1855

If you call out murder again I will split your head.

James Ashton and James Darby were brought up before magistrate Thomas Taylor, Esquire at Barnsley Court House, on Monday 21 May 1855, charged with highway robbery in Wentworth Park. Mr Whitfield briefly introduced the case by outlining events and then called the witnesses to support the charge.

Charles Berry, said:

I reside at Milton Iron Works, in the township of Hoyland, and am storekeeper to William Henry and George Dawes, ironmasters. I have been with them for the last five years and upwards. On the 5th of May instant, about eleven o'clock in the forenoon, I left the works in company with Robert Myers, to go to the bank at Rotherham, for money to pay the wages due that day. We went in a dog-cart and cream-coloured pony. Milton Iron Works is about seven or eight miles from Rotherham. We went through Wentworth town and through the park, the seat of the Earl Fitzwilliam. We got to Rotherham about twelve o'clock. It struck twelve when I laid the bag upon the bank counter. I went into the bank and left Myers in the street with the pony. I had occasion to come out of the bank to speak to Myers and to go with him shopping. After this, which would be about a quarter of an hour, I and Myers returned to the bank with the dog-cart and pony. I went into the bank leaving Myers at the bank door. I received my leather bag from one of the clerks in the bank. They did not tell me what was in it. It was weighty. When I left the bank somewhere about half past twelve, I put the leather bag in the bottom of the dog-cart, under the tool-mat. I and Myers got into the dog-cart, and Myers drove the pony. We had the articles we had purchased in the bottom of the dog-cart. On our return

*from the bank, Mr John Harrison passed us at a place called Greasbro'
Hill. He was driving. We moved to each other as we passed. In the
park there is a slight hill to ascend, and a planting on the right hand
side from Rotherham. The planting is about three or four yards from
the side of the road.*

Having described the location within Wentworth Park, Berry
then went on to relate what followed as the dog-cart made its way
up the slight incline. Two men, wearing caps, rushed out of the
planting, one was dressed in a green jacket, the other in a dark
frock coat. They took hold of the pony and brought the dog-cart to
a halt. Both men carried pistols and they called out in unison:

Deliver your money!

They repeated their demand for money, while keeping hold of the
pony's head.

Charles Berry said to them:

I have no money.

One of the men went over to the side of the cart where Mr Berry
was sitting and turned over the mat by his feet. On finding nothing,
the man went round to the other side of the cart, and pulled Myers
out of it. The other man then let go of the pony's head and joined
his accomplice. He pulled some shavings out of the cart and a pot
of honey. These were thrown aside and the cushion upon which
Myers had been sitting was removed, and the driving box beneath
was opened. Meanwhile, the other man was struggling with Myers.
Berry, called out 'Murder!' and the bigger of the two men, who it
was to be discovered later, was named Darby, told Berry:

If you call out murder again I will split your head.

Berry ignored this remark and once again called out 'Murder!'
Derby then went up to the dog-cart and, standing on the step,
struck Berry over the head, with a cane handle. Berry was wearing
a hat, and although he was shaken, he did not fall. Darby struck at
Berry's head again, which resulted in two severe cuts being sustained and considerable loss of blood. After this attack had taken
place Darby left the dog-cart and Berry drove off towards a nearby
lodge, leaving Myers and the two robbers behind. Berry said:

*I went towards the lodge, intending to go there. Blood was running out
of my Hat, and I turned into the main road, and asked a person to get*

Wentworth Woodhouse, the seat of the 5th Earl Fitzwilliam, situated in the heart of Wentworth park, where Charles Berry drove the dog cart and raised the alarm of the highway robbery. Keith Attack

into the dog cart with me, and we both went on to Wentworth House [Wentworth Woodhouse]. The money was all safe in the bag. When I was struck, I was standing on the rug under which the money bag was. I gave information at Wentworth House of the robbery, and I went to Wentworth to the surgeon, and got my wound dressed.

Robert Myers, said:

I reside at Hoyland, and am groom to Messrs Dawes of Milton Iron Works. On Saturday the 5th of May instant, I went with the last witness to the bank ... On the return journey, after we had passed Mr John Harrison at Greasbro' Hill and gone about a mile-and-a-half, and a planting near to it, and at this place two men came out ... they had each of them pistols in their hands ... They demanded our money several times. I said, 'We have no money.' The lesser man, who was on Berry's side, let go of the pony, and went up to Berry, and lifted up the mat. He did not say anything but came round to me. He again demanded the money. I said, 'We have none.' He then pulled me out of the dog-cart. I can't say where he seized me. I had one small box in my right hand breeches pocket, and 7s. 6d. altogether, also three keys in the same pocket. The lesser man pulled my pocket off, and slit my trousers, and took all away. He took the pocket pouch in my waistcoat pocket, with some tobacco in it; and also some ginger and a ginger grater. He threw me upon the ground and knelt upon me. He put a pistol towards my head and said, 'I will blow your brains out and cut your throat into the bargain, if you do not deliver up.' I said, 'I will deliver, if you will keep that damned thing off my head.' I was very much alarmed. After the struggle and taking my money, the bigger man ran across the park towards a pond leading to a wood. The lesser man then followed. I then went after both of them. I followed them 150 or 200 yards. They halted, seeing me following them. I looked round, but I could not seen anyone, except a woman a long way off. I came back again and I did not see them. I went to the place where the scuffle had been . . . I then went forward to Wentworth House. I was still stiff and sore with the man kneeling on me.

John Harrison, said:

I reside at Hoyland, and am a colliery agent there . . . I had occasion to go to Rotherham Bank, and when I got to a place called Cat-hill-lane Pond, which is on the way to Rotherham, I passed two men. After I had passed them five or six yards, one of them called out, 'Is this the road to Rotherham?' I looked round and noticed them and answered them, 'Yes.' I then went forward towards Rotherham, and, after doing business there, I returned, and passed Charles Berry and Robert Myers. They were in a dog-cart. I also passed them at the top of Carr House Hill, there was also Earl Fitzwilliam's postman, Abraham Parkin. In coming through the park, near to a tree, which is seated round, I passed the same two men which I had previously passed at Cat-hill-lane Pond. I did not speak to them, nor them to me. They passed me, one on each side of the grass. This would be about one o'clock.

Frances Falding, wood agent to Earl Fitzwilliam, said on Saturday 5 May, he was standing in Johnson's butcher's shop in Wentworth, close to the window-board, the shop being situated close upon the causeway. He noticed two men passing the shop and spoke to Johnson about them. They were going in the direction of Rotherham:

I am certain the prisoners are the men. I have not doubt whatsoever . . . I saw the prisoners this morning and picked them out.

The prisoners declined to say anything and reserved their defence. They were committed to York Castle to await their trial at the Assizes.

William Green, superintended of the Barnsley petty sessional division, said that on Wednesday afternoon, 8 May:

I apprehended the prisoner James Ashton. William Hirst was with me, he is one of the Barnsley constables. I found the prisoner at the Railway Tavern *beer house. I took him to the lock-up, and placed him in the passage along with another two men. I then sent for Charles Berry, and he identified the prisoner as one of the party who was concerned in the robbery of himself and Robert Myers. I then charged the prisoner with the robbery, and, in answer, he said 'What me! Not that. I am innocent of that lot.' . . . On Thursday morning the 10th instant, the prisoner James Darby was brought into custody by Joseph Swinbank, another of the Barnsley constables. I charged him with the robbery along with another man. He said, in answer, 'I am innocent. I would rather be hanged than locked up.'*

On the following day Berry and Myers identified Ashton and Darby as the two men who had robbed them.

George Airey, said:

I am the constable of Wentworth. On Saturday the 5th of May, I received information of the robbery in Wentworth Park, soon after one o'clock. I went in that direction and met Charles Berry and Robert Myers, and, from information I received, I went in search of the men. I received the articles, now produced, from Myers and Berry.

At the conclusion of the prosecution's evidence Mr Taylor said he had made his mind up to commit the prisoner's to the Assizes. However, he had no objection to hear the witnesses for the prisoners.

Mr Hamer said as counsel for the prisoners, he was sorry to hear that the magistrate had made up his mind before having heard his witnesses – witnesses of respectability and well known in Barnsley. However, having consulted the prisoners' friends, Mr Hamer informed the Bench that he had decided not to call any witnesses for the defence.

The prisoners were then committed to York Castle to wait their trial at the next Assizes. In July, twenty-six-year-old James Darby and thirty-four-year-old James Ashton, came up before Mr Justice Crowder, at the Yorkshire Summer Assizes, charged with assaulting and robbing Robert Myers in Wentworth Park, and also were charged with cutting and wounding Charles Berry, at the same time and place. Mr Hardy and Mr Maule appeared for the prosecution, Mr Blanshard defended Ashton, and Mr Price defended Darby.

The case for the prosecution was fortified by strong witness evidence, which clearly showed that Darby and Ashton were indeed the two men who held up Robert Myers and Charles Berry. As well as being identified by their victims, Darby and Ashton were also identified by several independent witnesses who saw them in the vicinity of where the robbery took place a short time before it occurred. Witnesses were called on behalf of Derby in an attempt to prove that he was in fact in Barnsley, some seven or eight miles away, at the time the robbery took place. Also in the case of Ashton witnesses were called in an attempt to prove that he was at the *Waggon*, a public house in Sheffield, some eight miles away, at the time of the robbery.

Replying for the prosecution, Mr Hardy submitted that the case had been clearly laid out. The identity of the prisoners had been satisfactorily proved by Myers and Berry, and there evidence was corroborated by several respectable witnesses. With regard to the alibis produced in the case of both prisoners, they were open to suspicion. In his summing up His Lordship paid great attention to the minuteness of detail in the case. The jury retired and returned with a verdict of 'guilty'. On Monday 16 July the prisoners were brought up before His Lordship for sentencing. Ashton was sentenced to six years' penal servitude, and Darby to four years' penal servitude.

CHAPTER 5

The Slaying of a Head Gamekeeper in Pilley 1867

... the professional poacher is, and will remain, a social outlaw ...

On the moonlit night of Wednesday 11 December 1868, one of the most sensational clashes within living memory occurred between poachers and gamekeepers near Pilley, at that time just a small hamlet situated in the township of Tankersley, about five and a half miles from Barnsley and eight miles from Sheffield. A desperate struggle took place and the poachers, armed not only with shotguns but also with bludgeons, had clearly been prepared to defend themselves against the possibility of being caught in the act. At the conclusion of this encounter, Lord Wharncliffe's head gamekeeper, George Thirkell, lay fatally wounded and another keeper sustained serious injuries. During the fracas Thirkell attempted to seize one of the poachers and, while struggling with him, another took aim with a gun and discharged it at Thirkell from a distance of about four yards, the charge entering his abdomen, causing injuries from which he died almost immediately.

When the news of the shooting reached Barnsley Police Superintendent Fisher a contingent of police officers set off for Pilley.

Thomas Oram's account was:

Thomas Maize, under keeper, James Hague, collier; and myself, met together a little before nine o'clock. All of us had sticks and Hague was carrying Thomas Maize's gun, which was a double-barrelled one. As we were going down Mr Gill's fallow field we saw two men getting out of the hedge which parted Mr Gill's field from that in which the affray took place. When the men got out of the hedge Mr Thirkell jumped over to them. The two men then began to run away. I followed Mr Thirkell

Lord Wharncliffe (Edward Stuart Wortley), 3rd Baron and later 1st Earl of Wharncliffe. Roy Young Collection

into the grass field, and we ran after the poachers. They began throwing stones at us. We over-took them and I knocked one of them down, while Mr Thirkell knocked the other down. They were running away towards the wood. With that the dog they had with them, and which had been beating about, came up, and we expected it would bite us. Mr Thirkell cried out to Maize, 'Shoot the dog'. Maize and Hague had jumped over the hedge after us. Maize shot one barrel at the dog but missed it. He then fired the other barrel, and the shot knocked the dog down. Mr Thirkell, who was nearest the wood, then left his man on the ground and came to me. I said to him, 'Look yonder gaffer, he's running away'. He ran after him 150 or 200 yards, and then said to Maize, 'Follow him on, I cannot run any further, and he can't go far.' Maize followed the poacher about 200 yards. Mr Thirkell then collared the man I had got down and we went towards the nets ... Maize and Hague were then both running after the other man towards the colliery. Mr Thirkell said to the man I had knocked down, 'Who is that man who has got away?' and he replied, 'I don't know.' Thirkell said, 'If you don't let us know I'll kill you.' By then the other men had got out of the dyke. I shouted, 'Look out gaffer,' and one of the poachers cried out, 'Shoot the bugger'. I saw one of them had a gun, and I knocked him down with my stick. He was pointing the gun at me at the time. One of the other poachers picked up his gun which had fallen from his hand. I then struck at one of the other poachers, and Mr Thirkell knocked one of the three others down. One of them hollered out, 'Shoot the bugger'. With that the poacher shot, this time at Mr Thirkell. And hit him. The one I had just knocked down had then got loose, and had gone along with the other poachers. He was bleeding very much, for I had hit him on the head. When I asked him what he had thrown stones for, and told him I had a good mind to knock his head off, he said to me, 'Pray you don't hit me any more'. All this time Maize and Hague were after the other. When the gun was fired Thirkell fell to the ground. I was then knocked down with one of the poacher's stick. I was struck on the head first, and they kicked me and hit me on the head and arms and body while I was on the ground. One of them called out, 'Kill the bugger,' and another said, 'Hit him on the head'. I hollered out and Maize and Hague came up. The poachers then gave over hitting me, and I managed to get up and run a bit off. As I was going, one of the poachers followed me and hit me several times across the back. As soon as he stopped hitting me I stopped and then went back to where Thirkell was. As soon as Maize and Hague came up the other poachers ran away. They went towards Pilley. It was quite moonlight, and I could see the men very well. Four of them were cut on their heads. There was a hare on the ground. The nets, which had been partly taken up when we came upon them, were left on the ground by the poachers. I saw the man I knocked down had a bludgeon, but my stick was rather the longest, so I got at him better than he could get at me. The poachers seemed to only have one gun with them, and it was that they shot Thirkell with. Our gun had been fired and had nothing in it when Thirkell was shot. He cried out, 'For God's sake Tom don't leave me. I am a dead man.' Maize raised him up in his arms and I then went away to Wiggin House, which is about 200 or 300 yards off. Stacey and another man got up, and came with me. I then went and called Mr Sykes up, and he sent his man for the doctor. As I was going back to the place a man met me and told me Thirkell was dead. We fetched the body away with Mr Sykes's horse and cart. When the poacher and me were scuffling together on the ground just after the beginning of the affray, I took some stones as big as pint pots out of his pockets. The stones would be intended to throw at us. He had also a live rabbit in his pocket . . .

The inquest was opened and adjourned on Friday 13 December, before Thomas Taylor, Esquire, the District Coroner, at the house of Mr Sykes, at Pilley, where a post-mortem examination had been carried out on the body of George Thirkell the previous afternoon. At the inquest it was heard that the post mortem was carried out by Mr Wainwright, surgeon, of Barnsley and Dr Watson, of Wortley. The gunshot had entered the abdomen about five inches below the naval at an oblique angle, causing severe damage to the bowel, which protruded from the wound. Such was the extent of the damage to the vital organs that there could be no doubt as to the cause of death. The deceased was an exceeding strongly built man and was possessed of a remarkably stable tenacity of muscle.

On Sunday 15 December the funeral cortege left the house of the deceased head gamekeeper, situated at the lower end of Holings Wood, a little after eleven o'clock. The procession was headed by eight young women attired in white dresses and bonnets. Then came the hearse bearing the body of Matilda Thirkell. Following this was a funeral bus, which as well as conveying the chief mourners to the church, also bore the coffin in which lay all that remained of the once powerful and stalwart George Thirkell. Then, walking two by two, were a number of the personal friends of the deceased, several farmers and the principal servants at Wortley Hall. Also in the procession were Dr Watson and J J Smith, Esquire, steward to Lord Wharncliffe. The bearers were all gamekeepers who had acted under the deceased man, namely Thomas Mayes, James Peacock, Joseph Woodcock, William Thornhill, William Brockwell and Robert Dixon. Among several other people processing to the church was Thomas Oram, who was with George Thirkell when the fatal shot was fired. All the children of the deceased, two or three of whom were very young, followed their sister's and father's bodies to their final resting place. The cortege arrived at St Leonard's Church, Wortley, shortly after the morning service had finished. The funeral service was conducted by the incumbent, the Rev G Brewin. During the committal proceedings at the graveside the grief of George Thirkell's little children was very intense, moving many of the spectators to tears. The funeral itself was a simple one, differing only from many others by the large number of people who followed the coffins to the grave. The general public also showed great interest in the proceedings. Some of those living further afield, curious enough to witness the sad event, were under the impression that the funeral and internment would take place later in the day. About forty people came over from Sheffield arriving on the one o'clock train. Several others arrived on foot but they were to be disappointed, because by the time they had arrived at St Leonard's Church, the internment had already taken place.

On Monday 6 January 1868, the magistrates sitting at Barnsley Police Court were the Rev H B Cooke and T E Taylor, Esquire, when Joseph English, Joseph Beardshaw alias Beecher and Matthew Cutts, were brought up charged with the murder of

George Thirkell. Mr Hamer appeared for the prosecution and at the request of the magistrates Mr Tyas watched the case for the prisoners.

The first witness to be called was James Haigh, miner, of Hoyland, who said:

In consequence of information I received, I went to the house of Thomas Mayes, a game watcher in the employ of Lord Wharncliffe, and told him what I had heard. This was communicated to the head keeper, Thirkell. Myself and Mayes left for a place called the 'Hollings'. I carried a double-barrelled gun, and Mayes had a stick. When we got to the 'Hollings' we were there met by Thirkell and another watcher named Oram. They both had sticks. We then together crossed some fields till we got to a footpath which led us to another field, which is occupied by Mr. Gill. Prior to going into the field we looked through the hedge, and saw two men, one of whom was engaged taking up a net. We walked along the footpath until we were opposite the two men, when Thirkell jumped through the hedge, and said, 'What are you chaps doing there?' and the rest of us followed. The two men began to throw stones, and Thirkell rushed at one of the men, and knocked him down. Oram did the same to the other man. Thirkell held his man down for about half a minute, and then came to Oram. Mayes and myself were there. We observed a dog coming towards us, and Thirkell said to Mayes, 'Take the gun, and shoot the dog'. Mayes took the gun from me, and shot at the dog, but the first barrel missed, and he fired again, and shot it. Oram then called out, 'Gaffer, your man's running away'. Thirkell then gave chase, and Mayes and I followed, he having given the gun back to me. We ran to the fence and jumped it. Thirkell ordered Mayes and me to follow the man, and he took the gun. We followed him to the Clayroyd bushes. We stood still for a short time, and heard something moving in the planting. We turned round and heard a gun-shot. It appeared to come from the field where we first saw the two men. We then heard Oram cry out, stick rattling, and immediately we returned to the field indicated. When we got to the fence we saw a man running. One ran across the field. The man returned and joined three other men, all of whom went towards the village of Pilley. They all jumped through the hedge. Going along the field we found Thirkell lying upon the ground. I went for assistance, leaving Mayes with him, and when I returned Thirkell was dead. The dog which was shot was a black one, with a white mark on its face and throat. The night was as light as day. I don't think I can identify any of the prisoners as being there that night. The dog produced is the dog I saw on the night of the murder. I know the prisoner Beardshaw but I cannot say that he was there on the night of the murder.

Thomas Mayes, a game watcher in the service of Lord Wharn-cliffe, in his own evidence corroborated that of James Haigh. In addition, he added:

When I got back to Thirkell he said, 'Oh, Tom, this is a bad job.' He then turned over and said, 'This is hard. Oh my poor family!' The last words he said were, 'The Lord have mercy on me!'

A gun was produced by Police Sergeant Elias Pilkington, which Mayes confirmed was the gun he had with him on the night of George Thirkell's death. Mayes then went on to say:

I went towards the hedge and found a hat, which I placed by the side of the body of Thirkell. I cannot identify any of the prisoners. I found the dog on the 13th December near the 'Hollings'. He was lame, and had shot marks upon him. One of the men (a little stiff man) had a velvet coat and a bald head. That was the man knocked down by Oram. I should know that man.

One of the prisoners, Cutts, was taken out of court and dressed in the clothes he was supposed to be wearing on the fatal night, but when he was brought back into court Mayes could not identify him. Gamewatcher Thomas Oram, gave the same corroborative evidence, then continued:

One of the poachers called out, 'Come up, Jack,' and began throwing stones. In the affray Mayes shot the dog and it screamed out. Mr Thirkell and myself knocked each a man down. Thirkell came towards me; I called out, 'Gaffer, the man is running away'. I was on the ground with my man for about ten minutes. I felt in the man's pockets and found a large stone, which I now produce. There was also either a live rabbit or a hare, and a bundle of net pegs [produced]. He was armed with a stick. I hit him on the head when I knocked him down, and his hat fell off. He had a bald head. He had a dark velveteen coat on and a round hat. Thirkell seized the man I had knocked down and said, 'Who is that man that has run away?' but the man said he did not know. While Thirkell was holding the man I heard some sticks crack, and then saw three men as if they were coming out of the ditch. I said, 'Look out Gaffer, they are here'. One of the three men had a gun. One of them said, 'Shoot the ******'. The man who had the gun *pointed it at me at a distance of two feet or a yard. I knocked him down with my stick. The prisoner Matthew Cutts is the man I knocked down, another man picked the gun up. The prisoner English is the man. I have no doubt of it. As soon as English picked the gun up, one of the four men said, 'Shoot the ******'. I then knocked another man down. I cannot say which it was. English put the gun partly up to his shoulder and shot George Thirkell. I saw him reel and fall to the ground. I was standing between English, the man who fired the gun, and Thirkell. After Thirkell was shot I was knocked down immediately. While on the ground I was both hit with sticks and kicked. The prisoner Beardshaw knelt upon me while the others were kicking me. While he was upon me one of the others said, 'Kill the ******', and another said, 'Hit him on the head,' and I was struck on the head. I called out for Mayes and he and Haigh came up to me. As they approached the poachers began to run away. When they left me I went towards Thirkell and asked him where he was shot. He replied, 'I am a dead man'. I asked him a second time, and he said, 'I am shot in the body'. Mayes and Haigh came up, and Thirkell said, 'Tom, don't leave me'. I then went away for assistance. I was away for a quarter of an hour or twenty minutes, and when I returned he was dead . . .*

The evidence of Dr Watson and the surgeon, Mr Wainwright, proved that the cause of George Thirkell's death was the result of the wound received in the affray. Mary Kitchen was the next witness to be called. She said:

I am the wife of George Kitchen, of Hoyland Common, beerhouse keeper. There are three rooms and a bar on the ground floor. I remember the day Thirkell was shot. I was at home. In the afternoon of that day Matthew Cutts came to my house. There was another man with him. It was about two o'clock in the afternoon. Later on in the day two more men came. It was after dark. I cannot swear to any of the men except Cutts.

Mrs Kitchen was reluctant to commit herself to identifying anyone other than Cutts, but with some gentle persuasion from Mr Hamer, she admitted that English was there as well as Cutts. Mrs Kitchen went on to say:

The two men who came after dark had nothing with them that I saw. All the four men were together in the kitchen. English and Cutts left first, and the other two in about half an hour. I did not tell my husband when I saw him next morning that Beardshaw had been at our house within an hour of the murder. I have not said within the last hour that Beardshaw was at our house on the night of the murder.

John Wilson, of Walworth Farm, Kimberworth, said:

I was at Blackburn, near Sheffield, between eleven and twelve o'clock, in the forenoon of 11th December last. Near to the Sportsman Inn *I saw Matthew Cutts and another man. I don't know the other man. They had dark clothes on, and each carried a bundle. They were going in the direction of Grange Lane.*

Witness Mary Handley, said:

I am the wife of a labourer at Brightside. I remember the 11th December, the day of the murder. Matthew Cutts was lodging at our house. The prisoner English called to see Cutts, and asked him if he would go for a walk. They went out together about ten o'clock in the morning. Cutts returned to our house between eleven and twelve o'clock. He said he had been on Hoyland Common in a row with the keepers, with Beardshaw and English. He said English had shot one of the keepers. I know John Barker's house at Attercliffe Common. I saw the prisoner Cutts after his apprehension, and in consequence of what he said I went to Barker's house for a gun. I received a gun from Mr Barker and brought it to my house. I afterwards gave it to Sergeant Pilkington.

Further information was exchanged before the proceedings were adjourned until the next day. On Tuesday the court was densely packed all day and outside a large crowd had gathered. As news of the evidence was revealed by those passing in and out of the court, it was discussed with great interest. Additional magistrates occupied the Bench: the Hon F S Wortley, H Otter, Esquire, of the Doncaster Bench of Magistrates; and Colonel Cobb. The first witness to be called was Police Superintendent George Ball, of the West Riding Constabluary, stationed at Bradford who said:

I know the prisoner Joseph Beardshaw. I apprehended him on 2nd instant, at Rocknook, Littleborough, in Lancashire, at half-past six in the evening. He was lodging with Ogden Smith. He was in the house. I said, 'You are Beardshaw; I want you for being concerned in the poaching affray near Barnsley, and murdering the head gamekeeper to Lord Wharncliffe.' He replied, 'Oh, that's a strange do, however.' I took him to the Littleborough Station. As were were going along he said, 'How long does it want to the assizes; about three months does it not? You might have let me alone a bit longerI should not have cared if I had got on to the assizes.' He said, 'Have they got the dog?' I replied, 'I don't know, but I think they have.' The prisoner said, 'I am not going to say I was not there – nothing of the sort. I was there right enough; its no good saying I was not. Of course they know I was; they could tell that by the dog.' I then took him to the lock up at Bradford, and when I got there I formally charged him with the night poaching, with a number of others, on the estate of Lord Wharncliffe, at Pilley, near Barnsley, on the night of 11th December last, and being concerned in the murder of the head keeper, Thirkell. Prisoner made no reply. On the following morning a communication was brought from Beardshaw to me. I went to the cell where he was and took him into the office. He said, 'Well, I have been considering it over, and I have made up my mind to tell you all about it how this affair occurred.' I said: 'Before you say anything it is only fair that I should caution you. You must understand that whatever you say to me, and no doubt will be given in evidence in evidence against yourself.' He said, 'Yes, I know that: I meant to say myself what I wish to say to you. I plead guilty to being there; but I am not guilty with anything to do with shooting or doing any bodily harm. I was three or four fields off when the gun was fired, and I did not know there had been anybody shot while I met a policeman on Attercliffe Common. He stopped me on the road and asked me my business. I told him I had been at Sheffield. The policeman asked me what time I left. I told him I did not know to an hour; he then said he had authority to stop everybody on the road, and ask them their business from Lord Wharncliffe. He said Lord Wharncliffe's head keeper had been shot. I am not going to be blamed for what someone else has done. There were four of us, Joseph Gregory, Joseph English, Matthew Cutts, and myself. We met at George Kitchen's, on Hoyland Common. We left there together, and put down our nets, not in the place where they came upon us. We set the nets at Woodside first, and then in the field where the keepers came upon us. It is a big field. Two of us, Gregory and I, put our nets on one side of the field, and Cutts and English set nets on the other side. The dog brought a hare to my net, and I killed it and threw it down. The dog went again and came back without anything. Gregory and I said to one another we thought we would take our nets up. I had took mine up all about ten yards when they came through the hedge with sticks. Gregory had a stick, but I had not. Thirkell came to me with a stick and hit me several severe blows on the hands, which were much hurt with guarding the strokes off. He then hit me on the head and struck me down. He 'frailed' into me after that. I told him I would get up and go with them, but he kept on beating me. He said, 'Get up –, or I will kill you'. I could not get up just then. I was laid on my belly. He got hold of me by the hair of the head and threw me right over. He said, 'I think thou art all right'; then he went away towards the net and Gregory. In a few minutes I came to myself, and raised my head up, when I saw them lifting Gregory up. I then jumped up and ran away, and when I had got a quarter of a mile away I heard a gun fired in the direction where I had come from. I have never seen any of them since. I don't know which of them had the gun. I did not see it.' As I was conveying the prisoner to Wakefield, he made a statement to me in the railway carriage. He said: 'There is one thing I missed telling you this morning. I said I did not seen the gun. I had forgotten; I did see it. I saw English lay it down when he began to set the nets. I don't know who took it up again. I know it was English's gun, because it was a double-barrelled one, and Cutts's is a single-barrelled.' Directly after he said: 'I suppose some of them had got my hat. I left it on the field.' The night I took him to the office at Bradford he complained about his finger, and asked that something might be done to it. It appeared to be broken, and he said he suffered great pain. I said: 'Have you had nothing done to them?' He said: 'No: I dare not go to anyone.'

Detective W Wetherill, then gave his evidence:

On the third instant I went to Retford and Newark, and there met Detective Hockaday and Sergeant Pilkington. We returned to Tuxford, and I there apprehended English. I charged him with being one of the parties concerned in the murder of George Thirkell . . . He in reply, said: 'I know nowt about it'. I was present when Hockaday searched the room. I saw him take up a rug, and in it was a gun bag folded together. He opened the bag and took out the gun. It was in two parts. Hockaday asked whose gun it was, and English said: 'It's my gun'. Before we left the house, prisoner said 'It was a bad job.' I took him to Doncaster. I there left him in charge of Hockaday.

William Lodge, labourer, of Pilley, said that on 15 December he was in a grass field occupied by Mr Pearson. Mrs Lodge said he found a large quantity of blood on the ground and about six feet away from the blood he found a loop belonging to the ramrod of a gun, which he gave to Sergeant Batty the same day.

Sergeant Elias Pilkington, of the West Riding Constabluary, stationed at Rotherham, said on 12 December he had gone to Carr

Brook, Attercliffe, at six o'clock in the morning, in order to search
for Joseph Beardshaw and Joseph English. He went to Beardshaw's house first but did not find him but he did find a gate net,
two purse nets, and nine net pegs, and a quantity of gun caps.
Sergeant Pilkington said he searched English's house during the
evening, where he found six net pegs and on 17 December he saw
Mary Handley, who handed him a gun, the property of George
Thirkell, the deceased head gamekeeper.

Joseph Hoyland, a coal-pit labourer, of Pilley, recalled that on
11 December he had seen English at Pilley at four o'clock in the
afternoon. He said he had known him for twelve or fourteen years
and that he was going in the direction of the colliery. Charles
Emmerson, butcher and beerhouse keeper, of Thorpe Hesley, said
on 11 December he noticed Matthew Cutts sitting in his taproom
drinking a pint of beer. His daughter, Elizabeth , also confirmed
Cutts was there, although she did not know him by name. She also
said Joseph English was also drinking there. Another daughter,
Sarah, also confirmed that Cutts and English were at their house
drinking. The Emmersons were the final witnesses of the day and
the case was adjourned until the following day.

On Friday, the Rev H B Cooke and T E Taylor, Esquire were
the sitting magistrates. Mr Sugg of Sheffield appeared for the
prisoners Beardshaw and English. Detective Samuel Hockaday,
stationed at Wakefield, was the first witness to be called. He
described how he and Inspector Wetherill had apprehended
English. Detective Hockaday said:

> When I found the gun I asked generally, 'Whose gun is this?' to which
> English replied: 'That is all right, it is mine'. I examined the gun and
> found that the two front loops crossing the ramrod were missing, and it
> was without a ramrod. It was full of earth and dirt, and the barrel and
> hammers were also full of dirt, in fact it was so in every part. I can not
> put it together in consequence of the dirt.

Barnsley gunsmith Thomas Steel, was the next witness to be
examined and he confirmed he had examined the gun and had
examined the loop found in the field and that it fitted the gun near
the muzzle end. Henry Hoyland, beerhouse keeper, of Attercliffe
Common, said he knew English, Cutts and Beardshaw. He said
English came to his house during the morning of 12 December. He
knocked him up and asked for some beer. English had a small cut
to his head. He asked Mr Hoyland to take care of his gun for him.

Wortley Hall, the seat of Lord Wharncliffe. Author's collection

Later that day, Cutts called at the house and Mr Hoyland asked him if he thought English was involved in what had taken place at Pilley, a question to which Mr Sugg objected. During further questioning Mr Hoyland said Cutts had replied in the negative. Aller Howe, of Canal Bank, Sheffield, said he had heard of something that had taken place at Pilley on 11 December. He went to Hoyland's public house, where he saw Matthew Cutts. He said:

> *I spoke to him and said his gaffer wanted him. I left him there but he followed me shortly afterwards to our house. He went out again with Mary Handley. He returned and brought with him a gun. It was in two pieces. He said he wanted to leave it there until it was called for. I said he was welcome. I gave it back again to Mary Handley two days after Christmas Day.*

Mr Hamer explained that the gun spoken of by this witness was not the one referred to by Detective Hockaday. William David Cliffe, sub-contractor, of Clumm Street, Sheffield said:

> *I know Joseph Beardshaw. I remember him coming to my house on the night of 11 December at twenty minutes before twelve o'clock. I got up*

and let him in. He was without hat. When he came in he said, 'We have been at Pilley and 'lit on' the keepers. Me and Jospeh Gregory was setting one side on the field, and a man of the name of Cutts and English was setting on the other side. They came onto us like lions; they knocked me down and I acted 'dummy'. They rushed on to Joe Gregory, and was beating him. I saw a chance of getting away, and I got up and ran away' He took a hare out of his pocket, and 'chucked' it on to the floor, and said they had shot his dog. He said they shot one barel at him and hit him, and he heard the keeper say give him the other. He added – 'By 'goe' Bill, if I had a gun in my hand I would have shot the big ******'. He said he should like to get away to the other side of Bradford, to his wife's friends, if he had got any money. He asked me to lend him a sovereign, and I lent him one, and also a cap. He had a velveteen coat and waistcoat on at the time . . . I kept the hare and cooked it. I did not notice that it was bruised out of the common way. I skinned it myself. It did not appear to be subject to blows or kicks.

Thomas Ellis, innkeeper, of Ecclesfield Common, said he had known Beardshaw for over twenty years. He said he remembered being at Sheffield with his wife on 11 December, and on returning home they overtook Beardhsaw and Joseph Gregory, at the floodgate, near Ecclesfield. They had a dog with them. Mr Ellis said:

I said to them, 'Hello, you have a little journey tonight I see'. Both of them spoke and said, 'Yes'. I said if you get a hare or two, and you have one to spare, I can do with it. Gregory said, 'If we get one; and have one to spare, I'll see thou has one'. They were on the turnpike road going towards Barnsley.

Hannah English was the next witness. She said:

I am the wife of William English, residing at Pilley. My husband is brother by the father's side but not by the mother's side to the prisoner, Joseph English. My husband's father resides at the Warren, Tankersley. I went to my husband's father's house on a Wednesday. I heard of the affray next day at Pilley. While I was there Joseph English, the prisoner, came in about ten o'clock at night. I opened the door, and when he came in, he looked as though he had been very ill-bruised. He had something with him, and he put it down by the door. He did not remain more than three or four minutes. After he had gone, I found a gun and some nets by the door. His father saw the gun and took it somewhere. I burnt the nets. In consequence of what someone said to me I went into the garden, and found a gun there buried, and brought it into the house, and placed it in the mangle.

Hannah Jagger, wife of John Jagger, of Clayton Heights, near Bradford, said:

I know Joseph Beardshaw. He married my daughter. I remember him coming to our house on Thursday 12 December last, in the afternoon. Whilst there I noticed his hands – one was swollen, and he was rubbing it. I asked him what it was done with, and he replied that he had been out poaching, there was another man with him, a bit off, when four keepers came and collared him and beat him with a thick hedge stake; they shot the dog; the first shot he screamed; they shot again; but he heard no more of him. He said Thirkell beated into him with his two-handed weapon. He held his hand up to stop the blows, and it was injured thereby.

At the conclusion of this evidence the prisoners were committed to the Assizes on the charges of murder and night poaching.

The resumed inquest was held at the *Wortley Inn* before Thomas Taylor, Esquire, on Monday 27 January 1868. Mr Hamer, solicitor, of Barnsley, was present on behalf of Lord Wharncliffe. Mr Sugg, of Sheffield, watched the case on behalf of the prisoners. John Jeffrestone Smith. At the conclusion of the evidence the jury returned a verdict of 'wilful murder' against Cutts, English and Beardshaw, as well as against a fourth man, Joseph Gregory, who was not yet in custody. With regard to the events in Pilley the *Barnsley Chronicle* reported on 11 January 1868:

Whatever difference of opinion there may be with respect to the game laws, which constitute one of the few surviving relics of feudalism, the professional poacher is, and will remain a social outlaw – one who sets at defiance both the statute law of the realm and the common law of nations ... That poachers are lawless and ready for any emergency, however desperate, we freely admit, but the law which prescribes their punishment also recognises their claim to be treated as human beings, and not as the wild beasts of the jungle. Keepers and watchers are not to use undue licence *because they are dealing with men who are* un-licensed, *and the sooner they are made to understand their duty in this respect the better.*

On 8 February, the *Barnsley Chronicle* reported news of an appeal to raise funds for the defence of English, Beardshaw and Cutts, and published the appeal letter:

Dear Friends,

This appeal is made on behalf of those unfortunate men who, on the night of the 11th December, were found poaching on the Warncliffe Estate, and during the excitement one of the keepers was shot. The men absconded, but have since been apprehended and are now in the hands of justice. Subscriptions are being raised to employ counsel on their behalf, and in order to mitigate their sentences; and also for the support of their wives and children, who are left destitute and without aid to support them. Any sum, however small will be thankfully received.

In addition to the appeal letter, the report also mentioned:

The amount of sympathy manifested for the men charged with being concerned in the murder of Thirkel, Lord Wharncliffe's gamekeeper, is almost unprecedented in the history of crime. Among the lower classes generally, and those of poaching proclivities in particular, it is believed the keeper provoked his own destruction, and efforts are being made with a view to retaining eminent counsel to defend them ... The following appeal is now openly posted in public houses in Rotherham and the vicinity of the murder, and it is said already substantial aid is promised.

Following the apprehension of Joseph Gregory and his subsequent appearance before Barnsley magistrates, the *Sheffield and Rotherham Independent* was moved to write in its issue on Saturday 22 February 1868 about the condition in which Gregory found himself following his encounter with Lord Wharncliffe's men near Pilley. Part of the article commented:

... It seems that Thirkell and his men might have secured them and disarmed them of their sticks without violence. But if we admit to giving to the keepers a licence the country would never permit to be assumed by the police in dealing with suspected thieves, or even murderers, that knock-down blows were the appropriate commencement – and a very severe blow one of them was, for it laid open Gregory's head by a wound long and deep, and stretched him bleeding on the ground ... And it must be remarked that all the punishment of Gregory was inflicted before Thirkell was shot ...

The trial of the three poachers Matthew Cutts, Joseph Beardshaw and Joseph English at the West Riding Assizes, was held at Leeds Town Hall on Saturday 28 March, before Mr Justice Hannan. Mr Maule, QC, Mr Hannay, and Mr Welby, conducted the case on behalf of the prosecution. Mr Forbes defended Cutts, Mr Vernon Blackburn, Beardshaw, and Mr Waddy, English. The fourth man convicted on the coroner's warrant, Joseph Gregory, was acquitted on the capital charge, as there was no evidence offered against him.

> *One great fact is that Thirkell met his death on the night of 11th December in a conflict with four poachers, and that, in some way or other, some one of these four men, whoever he was, caused the game-keeper's death. What the man was it is for you to consider. The evidence as to the direct identification rests solely on the testimony of Oram, and it was said, that he, for various reasons, is not to be relied upon unless he was corroborated by other independent evidence ... Weigh very carefully the statements made by various witnesses. Weigh very carefully the effect of the answers elicited by the Learned Counsel for the prisoners on cross-examination. It has been heard that the loops were sold by thousands and it is for you to say whether you are satisfied with the evidence provided by the gunsmith ... It is plain from the evidence that the design they had in view was poaching, and that they had no other idea than that of obtaining game by improper means ... You must take it from me that the keepers had a right to arrest the men engaged in poaching. The men set out with the intention of poaching. If they conceived the intention of making use of the deadly weapon they had in their possession in the event of them being obstructed in carrying out their purpose, or if they intended to use deadly weapons for the purpose of preventing their being arrested by the keepers, they would be guilty of murder, if in the use of the weapon they destroyed life. It is not necessary that there should be any deliberate or expressed agreement between the parties, but if during the course of the events they mani-fested agreement in any way in the use of the deadly weapon to prevent their being arrested, they would be guilty of murder, if one of them caused death. If you come to the conclusion that there was a deliberate intention in the minds of the man who use the words 'shoot him' to kill him, then he would be as much guilty as the man who did the act in consequence of what he had said. If the words were used merely to frighten and not to incite the other to shoot, then the man using the words would not be a participator in the act. It is for you to consider whether the man literally meant what he said. With regard to the violence which was said to have been made use of by the keepers, if in resisting this violence the gun of the poachers went off, then the offence would be one of manslaughter ...*

His Lordship's summing up lasted for some two hours. It included the reading of Beardshaw's statement. The jury retired and returned after about half-an-hour. The Clerk of Arraigns asked the inevitable question of the jury, if they had agreed upon their verdict. The foreman in reply said they found Cutts and English guilty of manslaughter, and Beardshaw not guilty. Beardshaw and Gregory were then further charged with poaching on the night in question, a charge to which both prisoners pleaded guilty.

Speaking on behalf of Gregory, Mr Campbell Foster addressed His Lordship. He said his client had pleaded guilty by his advice. He said on the night of Thirkell's death, his client was scarcely able to crawl home from the scene of the encounter, in consequence of the violence used towards him, and that for a long time his life was in danger. Mr Justice Hannan then proceeded to pass sentence. His Lordship addressed English first:

You have been convicted upon evidence which leaves no doubt upon the minds of anyone who has heard the case that the four of you in the dock were engaged in this poaching enterprise. You had with you a deadly weapon, but I am not sufficiently acquainted with the subject to know whether the place in which you had it threw any light on the motive you had in taking the weapon with you, but it is known that you went out engaged upon an unlawful business. You took a deadly weapon with you under circumstances that you must have known would be likely to bring you into conflict with the men whose duty it was to protect the game of their employers, and no man could possibly be engaged as you were on that night without knowing the great risk that you ran with having a deadly weapon with you. It is only in consequence of the merciful view which the jury has taken that I am spared the awful duty of passing sentence of death upon you. I greatly rejoice I am spared that pain, but still it is my duty to pass upon you [English] a sentence which will act as a warning on those engaged in similar pursuits and in the use of weapons likely to lead to fatal results. I therefore sentence you to ten years' penal servitude.

His Lordship then turned his attentions upon Cutts:

. . . who did not do the deed, I will pass a lesser sentence, but still one which will mark the seriousness of the crime of which you have been convicted . . .

Cutts was given a sentence of five years' penal servitude. His Lordship then addressed Beardshaw and Gregory:

Joseph Beardshaw and Joseph Gregory you have been acquitted of the more serious charge. Gregory, there can be no doubt that you were not a participator in the act. Beardshaw you have been acquitted by the verdict of the jury and therefore I have assented to it. I will not therefore assume that you were otherwise engaged in the matter, than as a poacher. I will make a slight difference in the punishment in consideration that Gregory seemed to have been hurt. I will sentence you Joseph Beardshaw to eighteen months' imprisonment with hard labour, and you Joseph Gregory to fifteen months' imprisonment with hard labour.

One of the prisoners in the dock was heard to mutter:

Thank you sir.

The four prisoners were then removed from the dock and the packed courtroom quickly emptied.

CHAPTER 6

Servant Girl Shot Dead by Thurlstone Publican
1888

Don't touch me, give me something to finish me, kill me right.

At a time when the whole of England was talking about the evil goings on that had recently occurred in the White-chapel district of East London, the sensibilities of the South Yorkshire public was alarmed to hear news of the tragic killing of another young woman that had taken place closer to home, on Monday 3 September 1888. On Tuesday 11 September, Henry (or Harry) Hey, thirty-six-year-old landlord of the *Blacksmith's Arms*, Thurlstone, appeared at Barnsley Court House, charged with the murder of his servant, Margaret Hill, a single young woman. The Bench comprised Messrs F H Taylor, J Dyson, R Inns, C Harvey, C Chapman and T Dymond. Mr John Carrington appeared for the prosecution and Mr H Horsefield, for the defence. The magistrates' clerk read the charge, which was:

That you, Henry Hey, on the 3rd September, 1888, at the township of Thurlstone, unlawfully, wilfully, and of malicious aforethought, did kill and slay Margaret Hill, against the peace of our sovereign lady the Queen.

In opening the case for the prosecution, Mr John Carrington, said:

In this case I am instructed to prosecute the prisoner at the bar, Henry Hey, who up to the day of this unfortunate occurrence, the 3rd of September, was an innkeeper and kept the Blacksmith's Arms *at Millhouse, near Thurlstone. The offence with which he is charged today, is, as you have just heard, that of causing the death of one Margaret Hill, a girl aged twenty-two years, on the 3rd of September of this year. The facts of the case are no doubt exceedingly painful, and* the details of the crime, from the terrible surroundings gathered from the evidence, may surely characterise this case as one of the most unfortunate your worships have ever had to inquire into.

There were several witnesses called to give evidence. Thomas Smith, a steelworker's assistant, to his father, of Bullhouse Grange, Thurlstone, said:

On Monday the 3rd September, I was passing the Blacksmith's Arms, *Millhouse, just before nine o'clock, and seeing a number of people standing in front of the house, and also observing that one of the front bedroom windows was broken, I called out in the direction of the broken window, 'Hello Harry'. I meant in so calling to call the prisoner. Shortly afterwards I saw the prisoner's head through the window, and he shouted to me, saying, 'Will you come in?' I replied, 'What is the matter?' and prisoner answered, 'I will tell you if you will come in'. I then went into the house followed by five or six other people, and as I was ascending the stairs, somebody said, 'Be careful, mind that he does not shoot you.' Prisoner heard the remark and said, 'I do not want you for that.' I then went into the front bedroom and saw the prisoner and a young woman, Margaret Hill. She was near the fireplace, either knelt down or in a crouching position, and the prisoner was behind her supporting her with his arms. I noticed some blood on the left side of the girl's dress. The prisoner on seeing me said, 'I have a sad job here.' I said, 'What have you being doing?' and he replied, 'I have shot the girl in the side.' I then went to Dr Wilson, of Penistone.*

Joseph Bardsley, school warden, of Thurlstone, said:

About five minutes to nine o'clock, on the morning of Monday, the 3rd September, hearing an alarm, I left the schoolroom at Millhouse, and went to the Blacksmith's Arms, *fifteen yards away. I entered the house along with Thomas Smith, followed him upstairs, and went into the front bedroom after him. When I got into the room, I saw the prisoner, Henry Hay, who was in a leaning position, and supporting the deceased, Margaret Hill, with his arms. They were between the fireplace and the window. On the floor beside the girl I noticed a pool of blood, and saw the deceased was wounded on the left side. I did not notice any other wound in the left side, but saw that her right arm was wounded in the elbow. I heard Thomas Smith speak to the prisoner, and he said, as near as I can remember, 'What have you done?' Prisoner replied, 'I've shot her.' I then went up to the prisoner and said, 'It is a sad job,' but I do not think he made any answer just then, but afterwards, looking towards me, he said, 'I shot her with the first in the arm. It did not do her, so I gave her the other, which I meant for myself. I had not another cartridge. My gun is there on the bed.' He pointed to it as he said so, and Mr Joseph Penn went to the bed and took up the gun. After this the prisoner made use of a lot of rambling talk to which I could give no meaning. To the best of my recollection, he said, 'I was obliged to do it; they were going to tear me to pieces and the children.' I do not remember anything more of what he said during the course of his rambling remarks.*

Joseph Penn, steel hardener, of Millhouse, Thurlstone, said:

Early on Monday morning, the 3rd September, I was in my own house when I heard the report of two gun shots, and a few minutes afterwards went to the Blacksmith's Arms, *which is close to my house. I went into the house and followed Mr Smith and Mr Bardsley upstairs. I went up into the front bedroom and saw the prisoner and the deceased. Prisoner was standing behind the deceased supporting her. There was a wound in the deceased's side, and her intestines were protruding through the wound, and through her clothes. Prisoner left the deceased when we*

The Blacksmith's Arms, *where Henry Hey shot Margaret Hill in 1888, seen here in the 1950s.* Old Barnsley

entered the room, and I asked her if I should lay her down, and she replied, 'Don't touch me: give me something to finish me, kill me right.' The prisoner at the time was sitting on the bed. I took possession of the gun, which was lying across the foot of the bed.

Arthur Cobden Jordan Wilson, physician and surgeon, said:

I knew the deceased, Margaret Hill, slightly, but do not remember her as a patient. On Monday morning . . . at about a quarter past nine o'clock, I was in my surgery, when Thomas Smith came for me. I went as quickly as I could with him to the Blacksmith's Arms. *I found the deceased lying on the bed, dressed, with her clothes laid upon her front. Prisoner was sitting in a chair in the corner of the room. When I was going to examine her, she said, 'O let me alone, I am in great pain.' And after that she did not say anything to me except to ask for her father and mother, saying, 'Have my father and mother come!' Prisoner talked a great deal to the people around him, but I did not pay particular attention to what he said.*

Police Constable Catherall, said:

At about half past nine o'clock on Monday morning, I apprehended the prisoner, Henry Hey, at the Blacksmith's Arms, *Millhouse, and took him to the police station at Penistone, and charged him with the wilful murder of Margaret Hill, by shooting her with a gun that morning. He said, 'Well, I don't know. I have had a bad wife.'*

At the conclusion of this evidence the prisoner was committed to take his trial at the next Assizes.

On Saturday 15 December, Henry Hay appeared at Leeds Assizes before Baron Pollock. Mr Banks and Mr C M Atkinson prosecuted and Mr J E Banks defended the prisoner. During his imprisonment at Wakefield, the prisoner had largely recovered his health and strength and during the progress of the trial appeared overwhelmed with shame. He wept bitterly at several times during the proceedings, particularly when his young son was giving evidence.

Mr Banks, in opening the case for the prosecution, stated the circumstances as proved in the evidence, and said the jury would doubtless be called upon to consider what was the state of the prisoner's mind. The witnesses would, all of them, speak of the conduct on the part of the prisoner which, apparently, showed that he was under some strange misapprehension, and Mr Wilson, the medical man, who was called in to attend the wounded girl, would doubtless be able to express his opinion on the subject. I will also call Dr Clarke, the medical officer of the prison in which the accused had been awaiting his trial and Dr Bevan Lewis, the medical superintendent of the West Riding Lunatic Asylum, who would state their conclusions for the benefit of the jury.

Thomas Smith and Joseph Bardsley were the first witnesses to be called. They gave their evidence along similar lines to that heard at the committal hearing.

Joseph Penn, steel hardener, of Millhouses, said:

I heard two shots, and then went to the Blacksmith's Arms, *and with Cardsley and others went into the upper room. Margaret Hill said, 'Don't touch me, give me something to finish me, kill me right.' Prisoner made several statements, one of which was to this effect – that he made deliberate aim at her, but he did not kill her, so he gave her the second barrel. He said he hadn't a third or he should have killed himself by placing it here, pointing it to his breast. Prisoner said the people in his street were punching his children about, and that if we went to the window we should see them. Prisoner made a number of rambling statements. He said he had to keep the gun by his side on the bed to protect him. He also said they had fixed a platform on the top of the stairs to shoot him. When he said they were punching his children, he added, 'Can't you hear them?' There were no cries of children at this time.*

Arthur C J Wilson, surgeon, said:

... the deceased was suffering from an abdominal wound, which was inevitably fatal, and a wound in the right elbow, which was smashed.

Mr Smith, who went on to describe the result of a post-mortem examination, then said:

I have known the prisoner very well for the last ten years, and had employed him. He was a good workman, and, as far as I could judge, of a peaceable and humane disposition. I had attended him several times. I attended him in January 1887 for delirium tremens. I did not examine him on this occasion, I heard him make rambling state-ments and mutter to himself. His appearance was that of a man in great excitement ... I considered he was suffering from delirium tremens, and was under delusions. It is a fact that upon each recovering attack of delirium tremens, the deliriums became stronger.

He had been two or three years in occupation of the public house. During that time he had been addicted to drinking; previous to that I had not known him to be an intemperate man.

Ben Hey, twelve-year-old son of the prisoner said:

I remember when Margaret Hill died, I got up that morning about six o'clock. My father came into the room before I got up, and he had his gun with him. I saw him again when I went to ask him for my school fees. Maggie Hill had breakfast with me that morning. I saw Maggie Hill take the powder-flask and shot up to my father's room. She said he kept bothering so for them. Just before she had finished breakfast she went upstairs. I followed her and saw her sitting down on a chair in the doorway. My father was sitting on the bed with the gun in his hand. The muzzle was pointed towards Maggie. He looked very wild. He was staring at a spot above the door. He said there was somebody coming. He kept saying, 'Sam, come out.' He had been saying it all the morning. He thought he was hiding somewhere. He also said, 'Sam, don't shoot me in front of my own son.' My father told me to take the gun from Sam. I tried to take the gun my father had, but he said, 'Don't take it from me, because he will shoot me.' I told my father there was nobody about, and Maggie Hill told him to be quiet. Maggie asked me to go downstairs. When I had been down about two minutes I heard two shots fired. I ran upstairs into my father's bedroom. Maggie Hill was kneeling on the floor, and my father fell back towards the bed. The gun was on the bed. He said, 'Oh, dear, Ben, I've shot Maggie.' He said he hadn't done it on purpose, that he thought she was some-body else. Maggie told me to go and fetch the doctor. The gun had been on the piano during the previous week, until Saturday. I took the pin out which fastened the muzzle and stock together, and kept it in my waistcoat pocket. Maggie told me where the pin was, and on Saturday he told me to put the gun together, and I did so . . . I took the pin out because my father said several times he would shoot himself. Maggie Hill had been our servant about nine months. My father and she appeared to be on good terms. I never heard any angry words between them . . . My father had been very poorly the previous week. On the Friday he was in bed all day, and I went to the doctors twice for him. On the Sunday night he looked very wild and seemed frightened. After the house closed he kept going about the house with me. He went in the cockloft because he kept thinking there was somebody there. He looked in every room in the house. I never heard anything at all and he kept telling me to listen. He kept looking up as if he heard the noises above his head. My mother slept with Maggie that night in Maggie's bedroom. I heard him tell my mother and Maggie on Monday morning that he had seen some things in the night. He said they had been wheeling my mother about in a wheelbarrow. On Sunday he said he had seen my grandmother on a barrel in the kitchen, and when he went to look at her there, there was nothing but a pile of rags. He also said he saw some cats on the sink, and then they turned into a cat's head and a dog's. He said, too, that it was a nice looking baby, but it became right foul.

Dr Henry Clarke:

I first saw the prisoner on the 9th September. He was then practically convalescent. I have heard the evidence given in court. Are you in a position to any opinion as to his mental state on the 3rd September? Very clearly. – Are you able to say whether he was suffering from any known form of mental disturbance at that time? Unquestionably – What form? Delerium tremens – That is a form of insanity almost invariably accompanied by delusions, is it not? ... These delusions often relate to the identity of particular persons. – They sometimes confuse, perhaps, a near and intimate friend with some enemy. I made a report to the Public Prosecutor. I made that report partly from information I received from the assistant medical officer of the prison, and partly from what I saw myself. Widely dilated pupils, general muscular tremor, especially of the tongue, and profuse perspiration, are all objective symptoms of delirium tremens. And this condition cannot be feigned in its entirety.

Dr Bevan Lewis, resident medical officer of the West Riding Asylum, Wakefield, said:

I examined the prisoner on the 5th November, and after hearing the evidence today I am able very clearly to express an opinion as to his mental condition on 3rd September. In my opinion he was suffering from delirium tremens.

Cross-examined by the defence:

Does the shock and horror of a deed like this sometimes produce a temporary return to reason?

Dr Bevan Lewis, in his reply to this question, said:

This is a well known and established fact.

In his summing up, His Lordship said:

I need hardly tell you it is a proposition of law that every person is responsible as a rule for the natural consequences of his own act. If it be made to the jury to appear that at the time the act was committed the prisoner had not the power of judgement between right and wrong and was affected by insanity in that sense, although he might in one sense be guilty of the offence – guilty of the act – he is not guilty of the crime which the law would attribute to a man who was of sane mind. In such cases the mode of procedure, regulated now by statute, was that if the jury comes to the conclusion that the person who committed the offence was of unsound mind, then it is your duty to so to find. In the present case there can be no doubt whatever that the prisoner committed the offence, and the next question is, was he of unsound mind at the time? I understand you have no doubt upon that question. I think you could not possibly have any when you consider the evidence – a class of evidence which you do not always get in theses cases – of those who knew the prisoner before the act, those who saw him after the act, and were able to notice his conduct and demeanour from time to time, coupled with the skilled evidence of medical men who are conversant peculiarly with this subject, and who told them what was not their mere opinion, but their absolute conclusion on these facts. If you adopt that view, it will be your duty to say that the prisoner is guilty, but at the time of the commission of the offence he was a person of unsound mind.

The jury retired to consider their verdict and returned after an absence of ten minutes, when the foreman delivered the verdict:

Guilty, but at the time of the commission of the crime he was in a state of unsound mind.

His Lordship directed that the prisoner should be detained until Her Majesty's pleasure be known. Henry Hay looked somewhat relieved as the verdict and sentence were given and he was immediately removed from court.

CHAPTER 7

Murdered in a Caravan in Handsworth Woodhouse 1889

I've killed her. Come and look she's dead in the wagon ... Go and have a look.

Forty-five-year-old Robert West, who was born in Oxford, had been a travelling showman all his life. The *Sheffield Telegraph* described him as a very determined fellow with a firmly set face that wore an expression of fierceness; he looked half-gypsy, half-horse dealer. Brought up on the road, travelling from fair to fair and feast to feast, in recent years his Aunt Sally stall, shooting gallery and swing boats, had become a familiar site throughout the Midlands and parts of Yorkshire. For several years he lived with a woman named Houlden, and she bore him three children. After her death he took up with the daughter of another shooting gallery owner, in Derby, and despite the girl's mother's dislike of her prospective son-in-law, Emma Sketchley, who was fourteen years younger than West, married him in 1877. In 1883 their first child was born and two more followed.

The West's travelled with two vehicles, one being a two-compartment caravan for living in, comfortably fitted out with bunk beds and reminiscent of the type of cabin one might find on board an elegant steam ship of the day. The other vehicle was specially adapted to take the three fairground attractions. The Wests invariably travelled with two other showmen: Charles Warwick, Robert West's brother-in-law, who was married to Emma's sister, who ran a photographic van, and the West's long standing friend, Thomas Twigdon.

The first rift of what was to become a regular feature between Robert and Emma West, came late in 1888. It was at the Handsworth Feast that year that someone tipped West the wink that his wife was deceiving him, allegedly with a showman named John Baines, more commonly known as 'Leicester Jack'. West tackled his wife about this allegation but she denied there was any truth in it. Clearly he was not convinced that this was the case and relations soured between them. When he was drunk, which was all too often, the subject of his wife's infidelity inevitably came up and he regularly hit her. On occasions he had even threatened to kill her. In the Summer of 1889, while they were in Derby, matters came to a head, as West once more accused Emma of infidelity. He was arrested and the following morning appeared before the town's magistrates charged with assault and using obscene language. Emma came to her husband's defence, trying to get the charges dropped but he was convicted and fined 30*s* – or in default six weeks' imprisonment. Emma paid the fine herself to prevent her husband's incarceration. Although she returned with him to their caravan, her mother persuaded Emma to leave West and go and live with her.

After a few weeks Emma went out on the road again with her brother-in-law, Charles Warwick, but fairs being what they are, it was almost inevitable that they would meet up with West again on the road, which they did, in early August, at a fair at Riddings in Derbyshire. They agreed to a reconciliation and West promised to behave better in future. So, the Wests settled down to travelling on the road again together, but it was not long, only a matter of days in fact, before Robert West's jealousy surfaced again and the rows returned. By the second week in August they were at Clay Cross and during a row there West once again threatened to kill his wife, which prompted Emma to tell her friends and travelling companions:

It's only the drink. I think the world of him and he would never hurt me.

The Wests moved from Clay Cross to Handsworth Woodhouse on Friday 16 August, in readiness for the Woodhouse Feast, a gig Robert West had done for years, and he habitually pitched his caravan in a field adjoining the *Royal Hotel*. When the first van reached Dronfield, West told Emma to carry on to Woodhouse and pitch the caravan in Hawkesworth's field, while he went on to make some purchases in Sheffield.

When West arrived at the caravan at Woodhouse at about 9.30 pm, in a cab, he was somewhat inebriated. After checking on

The market cross, Woodhouse. The Royal Hotel *was where Robert West was drinking on the night he murdered his wife.* Old Barnsley

the caravan he went to the *Royal Hotel* before moving on to the *Cross Daggers*. In the latter, where he stayed until closing time, West struck up a conversation with a showman named Benjamin Law. West was slumped on the table with his head in his hands. When Law asked him what was the matter, West replied:

> *Oh Benny you don't know. Benny I shall do the bitch tonight if they start of me.*

While West was out drinking his wife was in her sister's caravan attending to her needs, as she was unwell. Emma left her sister at closing time and went off to meet her husband, returning with him to their own caravan. As West went into the caravan his wife remained outside talking to Thomas Twigdon. After a few minutes West came out and said:

> *Emma are you coming to bed?*

She replied that she would be in in a minute and West said good-night to them both. Emma West joined her husband in the caravan after a few minutes and Thomas Twigdon returned to his own caravan, which was pitched nearby. At 5.30 am Twigdon was awakened by a knock on his door. When Twigdon opened the door he was confronted by West, who asked him if he would get up, to which Twigdon replied that it was too early. West's earnest reply was:

Oh, but do get up I have something particular to tell you.

When Twigdon asked what it was all about West simply replied:

Tom, I've killed my wife.

Wigden was disinclined to believe West, who reiterated:

I've killed her. Come and look she's dead in the wagon. She's in the wagon. Go and have a look.

Twigdon would not do as West asked but asked him how he had done it, to which West replied that he had cut her throat. He admitted that he had done it soon after she had entered the caravan. Twigdon made the decision to go and fetch Charles Warwick. Before they entered the caravan West said to Twigdon and Warwick:

I want both of you to go with me to the police station first and I'll give myself up.

However, when they arrived at the police station all the officers were out on their beats, so all three returned to Hawkesworth's field. Warwick suggested that they check to see that Emma West was really dead. When they looked in they could see the bed was covered with blood. Emma West was lying on the bed, dressed in her night clothes, with her throat cut. Alarmingly, sleeping next to her was her young child, totally oblivious to its mother's condition and its night clothes spattered with its mother's blood. Warwick gently picked the child up and removed it to his own caravan.

When Warwick returned he asked West why did he do it, to which question West replied that they had had a row and the result was that he had jumped out of bed and slit her throat. Soon afterwards Police Sergeant Ford, who was about his normal duties and totally unaware of the events at the West's caravan, came up to West who was sitting on a wall, and West said to him:

I have done it. You can take me and lock me up or do what you like with me.

Sergeant Ford, believing that West was joking with him told him to go home as he was not sober, to which West replied:

Sober or not, I have killed her.

At this juncture Twigdon and Warwick appeared on the scene and confirmed the awful truth. Having briefly looked into the caravan, Sergeant Ford sent for help to the station and also for Dr Pillow. When the doctor arrived he confirmed that the woman was dead and had been so for some time. Soon afterwards West was taken to the police station. On his way there West said:

This thing has been brewing twelve months. It will be next Sunday twelve months when we were here for the Feast last year when I began to find out her tricks. There's another I intended to do first. That Leicester Jack and then her but the bugger kept out of my way. I should have put his lights out first.

On arrival at the police station he was charged with murder. When Police Superintendent Midgeley arrived he arranged for the caravan to be removed from the field into the yard of the *George Inn*. Emma West's body was taken inside the inn for a post-mortem examination in preparation for the inquest.

At 8.00 am on Sunday morning West was taken by rail to Sheffield and transferred to the Central West Riding Police Office in Burngreave Road. On the journey there he said he did not wish to live any longer and he wished he could be finished off that day.

The inquest was held at the *George Inn*, Woodhouse, on Monday 19 August, before Coroner Dossey Wightman, Esquire, at 2.45 pm. The foreman of the jury was William Birks. Robert West, who had been brought there by cab, was seated in the corner of the room, well away from the windows. A large crowd had gathered in the street outside. The entire proceedings lasted under two hours, the coroner having declared that this was the simplest case of murder he had had to deal with during his long coroner-ship.

Dr Henry Pillow, surgeon said:

About 6.30 on Saturday morning, I was summoned by Sergeant Ford to see the body of the deceased at Mr Hawkesworth's croft. It was lying on the bed in the van. Deceased was dead, and in my opinion had been dead about five hours. I examined the throat, and found a gaping incised wound on the left side, extending from the ear downwards, and forwards to the middle line of the neck, below the larynx. The windpipe was not injured, but the carotid artery and jugular vein were severed. That caused death. It was a wound which might possibly have been inflicted by the deceased herself. Judging from the evidence I have heard, however, I should think that is improbable.

A long altercation took place between West and his mother-in-law, in which West said that it was she who was the cause of it all. At the end of the proceedings the jury returned a verdict of wilful murder against West and Mr Wightman signed the committal warrant.

On Tuesday 20 August the *Sheffield Daily Telegraph* reported:

The sensation produced on Saturday at Handsworth Woodhouse by the discovery of a horrible murder in a showman's van had by no means subsided yesterday. On Sunday thousands of persons visited the locality and thronged the spot where West's caravan had stood. No signs of the tragedy remained, but a morbid interest kept people about the scene, discussing the murder from many points of view.

Also on Tuesday there was a committal hearing before magistrates Sir Henry Watson and T W Cadman, Esquire. West sat with his arm resting on the brass dock rail and his head in his hand, throughout the proceedings and maintained an air of disinterest. Although from time to time he moved in recognition of old friends. Again there was a clash with his mother-in-law, during which she said to him:

You bad man, you murderer, you villain. You ought to have your neck stretched.

West replied:

You caused three parts of it yourself. You have no occasion to blame me. Blame yourself. I have done it and I am very glad of it. I want to die, that is what I want. I am glad I have done it. I told you a long while ago I should do it and I have meant to do it.

Mrs Sketchley then said to West:

Villain! Blame yourself not me. And Leicester Jack. You and him that is the two.

The altercation continued and it became necessary for the Bench to order Mrs Sketchley out of the witness box. At the end of the proceedings, having been committed to take his trial at the Assizes, West called out to his friends in the courtroom, who included Charles Warwick and Thomas Twigdon:

Goodbye all of you.

On Wednesday 21 August the funeral of Emma West took place in Derby. The procession, consisting of the hearse and seven Broughams, left the *White Horse Inn*, Morledge, at 2.30 pm, Mr Samuel Sketchley, the deceased's brother's public house. The coffin had been brought there on Monday night. The funeral was conducted by Mr Thomas Lloyd of London Street, Derby and officiating at the graveside at Nottingham Road Cemetery, Derby, was Primitive Methodist minister Mr William Marwood.

Robert West's trial took place at Leeds on 14 December 1889, before Mr Justice Manisty. Mr G J Banks and Mr W W Thompson appeared for the prosecution and Mr L A Kershaw and Mr Palmer appeared for West. There being not the slightest doubt that West had murdered his wife the defence based its case on the prisoner's insanity. Thomas Twigdon in his evidence said that West suffered a bad attack of brain fever some seven or eight years before the event and had been told he should never drink. Twigdon said that up until 1888 West and his wife appeared to be very happy together but after he discovered about Leicester Jack West began to brood.

The defence called only one witness, the prisoner's sister, Fanny Cooper. Mrs Cooper said that many family members had suffered from insanity. The prisoner's grandfather had been insane and had been incarcerated in an asylum at Abingdon until his death. His great uncle had to be strapped down to his bed because of insanity and a cousin also suffered from insanity. Mrs Cooper admitted that she had not seen her brother for twenty years but said that when she had known him he displayed the same signs of insanity as other members of her family.

Mr Kershaw, addressing the jury, said:

There is not the slightest doubt that the prisoner murdered his wife but I must ask you to say that it was done in a moment of insanity, his blood having been raised to a pitch of excitement by long brooding over the ills which had been wrought to his domestic peace by Leicester Jack. It was at Handsworth where his peace of mind was first destroyed and on returning to the place after an absence of twelve months, it is not difficult to understand that the germ of insanity within him was roused by the terrible thought of the wrong that had been done to him and sprang into full being in one round. Reason for the time being was thrown from her seat and the prisoner for the time being was in the grasp of an insane impulse – an impulse which he followed blindly to whatever end it might tend. In the present case the man's hand turned against the one whom he loved best in the world, and I would remind you that prior to the time when he began to doubt the fidelity of his wife he loved her, as you were told by Twigdon, more than life.

For the prosecution Banks submitted that the evidence brought by the defence did not show that the prisoner was insane, and supposing every word spoken by Mrs Cooper was true, there was no evidence to show that West had been otherwise than perfectly sane for the last twenty years. In his summing up, Mr Justice Manisty directed the jury that drunkenness was no excuse for the prisoner having committed a crime, and also there was no evidence of apparent insanity in the prisoner, though no doubt there was evidence of insanity in the family.

The jury retired to consider the evidence and returned shortly with a verdict of guilty, with a strong recommendation to mercy on account of the great provocation he had received. As was customary, His Lordship donned the black cap, then told West:

Robert West, you have been found guilty of the murder of your wife. It is not for me to make any observations on the heinousness of that crime. The law imposes on me one duty and one only and that is to pass sentence of death.

Robert West did not receive a reprieve. He resigned himself to his fate and while he awaited his execution he was attended by the prison chaplain at Armley, Rev Dr Bowlam. He was hanged by James Billington on 31 December 1889, together with a thirty-nine-year-old Halifax murderer, Frederick Brett.

CHAPTER 8

Murder of a Police Constable in Piccadilly
1900

... stepped back two paces, pointed the revolver at Police Constable Kew, and fired.

On Tuesday 10 July 1900, the brothers Charles and Frederick Backhouse had been drinking in Parkgate, and earlier Charles had acquired a revolver and ammunition. They returned to Piccadilly, the hamlet where they lived, on the outskirts of Swinton, and continued on their drinking binge at the *High House* public house there. Police Constable Kew, who lived near to the Backhouse brothers at Piccadilly was informed that they had a revolver in their possession.

Police Constable John William Kew was born in Langton, near Horncastle in Lincolnshire, on 9 February 1871. He worked as a farm labourer until he was twenty-one, then joined the Lincolnshire Constabulary. Two and a half years later, he transferred to the West Riding Police, initially working with the Pontefract Division. In August 1896, Kew commenced work at the new Swinton Police Station, and moved to a police house at Piccadilly in March 1897, becoming the first police officer to be posted there, which at that time was more remote from Swinton than it is in the present day. As well as Picadilly and part of Swinton his beat included Warren Vale.

In the closing years of Victoria's reign Piccadilly was regarded as being a 'rough area', and locals from adjacent areas would refer to the rough and ready lot and smattering of sometimes notorious characters at Piccadilly as those living 'on t'hill'. Police Constable Kew soon gained the respect of local residents and he, his wife and four children, became part of the local community. The Backhouses were well known to Police Constable Kew and they were

The High House *public house, Piccadilly, today.* The author

generally regarded locally as being part of the rough and ready fraternity. On Monday 9 July 1900 Frederick, commonly known as Frank, the younger of the Backhouse brothers, was summoned to appear at the Rotherham West Riding Police Court, charged with having assaulted his brother's wife, Gertrude. He was fined 40*s* and costs in his absence. Gertrude Backhouse came from a well-known Piccadilly family, the Kemps and Charles and Gertie Backhouse had one child, Ethel.

On the night the tragedy occurred, Tuesday 10 July, at about 11.30 pm, having learned that the Backhouse brothers had a loaded revolver in their possession, Police Constable Kew, the only police office stationed at Piccadilly, approached Charles and Frederick Backhouse, as they were standing in a yard by the house where they lived, the younger man, Frank, being a lodger with his brother. There was a brief conversation concerning the amount that the magistrates had ordered Frederick Backhouse to pay, and Frank Backhouse, using an assortment of expletives said he wasn't going to pay, then, according to witnesses, Charles Backhouse stepped back two paces, pointed the revolver at Police Constable Kew, and fired. The bullet struck the constable in the chest.

Police Constable William Kew. Giles Brearley Collection

Immediately afterwards Charles Backhouse handed the revolver to his brother, who promptly fired a second shot at Constable Kew, wounding him in the thigh. Constable Kew was a tall, powerfully-built man, and he had grasped hold of the older Backhouse, Charles, and despite his injuries maintained his grip and dragged him up the passage towards the police office, Constable Kew's own house, and eventually Charles was secured and taken indoors. Several residents alarmed by the shots sent for help.

Dr Fullarton was quickly in attendance, and Sergeant Danby, in charge of Swinton Police Station, Sergeant Ball and Police Constable Yates, of Kilnhurst, were soon on the spot and took the Backhouse brothers into custody. Frank Backhouse had remained outside Constable Kew's house with the crowd. He was told the police had been sent for and he would probably be arrested, but he remained on the spot, declaring that he would not run away. On his arrival Sergeant Danby put his hand on Frank Backhouse's shoulder and spoke to him. Frank produced the revolver from his pocket, holding it in his right hand. Seregeant Danby then took the revolver from him and placed him in custody. The Backhouse brothers were taken to Swinton Police Station and they were removed from there to Rotherham Police Station on Wednesday morning. Meanwhile, Constable Kew was assisted to bed, where the doctor remained in attendance. The first bullet had entered the left side of the chest about an inch below the heart. The second bullet caused a wound in Constable Kew's left thigh. Constable Kew remained conscious for the greater part of the night but lapsed from time to time into unconsciousness. On Wednesday morning it was decided that he should be taken to hospital, where the Rontgen rays appliance could be used to extract the bullets. During the early morning before his departure for hospital, Constable Kew was visited by several neighbours, including Mrs Backhouse. He was able to speak to them. At 11.00 am an ambulance was procured from Warren Vale Colliery. Many of those who saw Constable Kew being carried out of the house to the ambulance, on seeing how pale and exceedingly weak he appeared, expressed the opinion that he would not return home alive again. The painful journey to the Rotherham Hospital lasted over an hour and the gravely injured policeman was admitted at 12.20 pm. He underwent X-ray examinations to locate the bullets but he succumbed to the wound to his chest and died at about 2.10 pm that same afternoon. He was twenty-eight-years-old.

The inquest was held before Coroner Dossey Wightman, Esquire, on Friday 13 July, in the waiting room of the Rotherham Hospital. The jury brought in a verdict of wilful murder against the Backhouse brothers, and they were committed for trial on a coroner's warrant. Following the inquest proceedings, William

Kew's body was conveyed from the Rotherham Hospital to his home. On Saturday 14 July, at two o'clock, the mournful funeral procession began and made its way to St Margaret's Church, where a service was conducted by the Rev W J Peacey, Vicar of Swinton, and afterwards Police Constable Kew was buried in the churchyard. His coffin was borne to the grave by uniformed members of the West Riding Police Force.

Dossey Wightman, Esquire (1836–1920), solicitor and partner in the Sheffield firm of Wightman and Parker. He was the coroner who presided over the inquest. Author's collection

On Monday 16 July a large crowd of people gathered in Rotherham's College Square outside the Rotherham West Riding Court, where the brothers appeared on a charge of wilful murder. A second committal hearing was heard there on Wednesday 18 July. On 27 July the Backhouse brothers were tried in the Crownt Court in the Town Hall at Leeds Assizes, before Mr Justice Ridley. Mr Harold Thomas prosecuted, and the prisoners were defended by Mr E A Mitchell Innes.

Charles Benjamin Backhouse, aged twenty-three and Frederick Lawder Backhouse, aged nineteen, were indicted that they feloniously and wilfully and with malicious aforethought did kill and murder John William Kew, at Piccadilly, Swinton, on 10 July 1900. Mr Harold Thomas detailed the case for the prosecution at some length.

Thomas Brazier, ironmonger, of Rawmarsh, with business premises at Parkgate, stated that Charles Backhouse purchased from him a revolver and nine cartridges. When Mr Brazier was wrapping up the revolver he asked Backhouse if he was after some cats and Backhouse replied, 'No.'

Dr J Sackville Martin, house surgeon at Rotherham Hospital, gave evidence concerning Police Constable Kew's injuries, stating that had only the second shot been fired, the man, in his opinion, would have lived. During cross-examination by Mr Mitchell Innes the following exchange took place:

> Mr M Innes: *I take it as your opinion that the man would have died had the hip wound not been inflicted?*

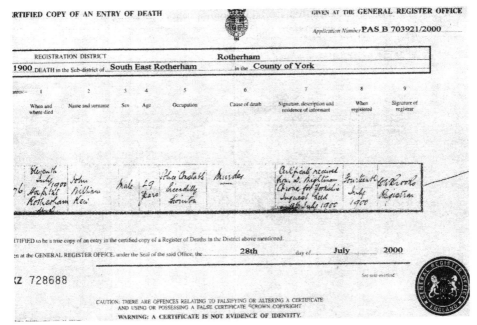

William Kew's death certificate. Giles Brearley Collection

Dr J S Martin: *Yes.*

Mr M Innes: *Was there any blackening due to powder?*

Dr J S Martin: *Yes, near the wound in the abdomen.*

Mr M Innes: *In your opinion was the pistol fired at close range the first time?*

Dr J S Martin: *Yes.*

Mr M Innes: *What would you call close range?*

Dr J S Martin: *Anything within six yards.*

Mr M Innes: *Was there any blackening about the wound on the hip?*

Dr J S Martin: *No.*

Several other witnesses were called who gave evidence of events preceding the shooting and the shooting itself.

Mr Harold Thomas summed up the case for the prosecution, pointing out in regard to the police proceedings for assault against Frederick Backhouse that Kew was the person whose duty it was to serve the summons, and, in case he did not pay the fine ordered, to arrest Frederick in default. Mr Thomas said he thought it might fairly be assumed the men were away from home the day the summons was heard on account of some matrimonial differences that

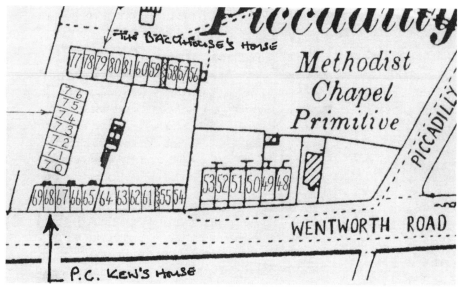

Map showing the site of the murder, which took place in the yard between Police Constable Kew's and the Backhouses house. Giles Brearley Collection

Piccadily in the present day. This view shows numbers 48–53 Wentworth Road. The houses are similar in style to No 68, the home of PC William Kew. Numbers 69–54 have been replaced by modern housing. The author

had taken place within the house of Charles. The prisoners meant to use the weapon upon some person or other ...

Mr Thomas continued:

What was Charles doing with the pistol in his hands at all? If it was in his pocket merely for an innocent purpose, on the constable saying, 'I am entitled to search you,' would it not naturally be supposed that he would have asked the reason for the search? Instead of that, Charles, without a single word of explanation, and without asking Kew why he was there, put his hand in his pocket merely for an innocent purpose, shot him ... If the pistol had been purchased for an innocent purpose Charles would never have produced it and shot the constable.

Frederick, Mr Thomas pointed out, made no attempt to stop his brother. He said if the jury thought the affair was an accident they should acquit him, and also Frederick if they thought he stood by merely as a spectator and was not an aider and abettor; but if they were satisfied both were concerned and that one delivered the fatal shot, he submitted that they should return a verdict of wilful murder against both of them.

Mr Mitchell Innes, addressing the jury for the defence, said:

It now becomes my duty to address you on behalf of these two men, who are charged before you today with the gravest, the only capital crime known today to our law. An inquiry into murder must always be painful, and perhaps in this particular instance that painfulness is not lessened by the fact that there are two men whose lives hang in the balance of your decision. But however painful it be, I for one must

A present-day view of the site of the shooting of Police Constable Kew. The author

begin what I have to say by saying that nothing could have been fairer, more impartial, and more apt to conduce to a fair verdict being arrived at by you, than the way in which the case for the prosecution has been conducted by my learned friend. As a rule, in cases of this character, you are judges to the facts and nothing else as between the two men are concerned; but there are instances, and this is one of them, in which the law and the facts are so intermingled that in order to properly compre- hend the law of the case and appreciate what may be urged in defence of the prisoners it is necessary to touch upon the legal aspect of it . . . Now I begin with saying with regard to the legal position of the prisoners – and I say it without fear that I shall be upheld by His Lordship – that if the prisoner Frederick had been charged alone in this dock today with the murder of Kew, and if the evidence and the medical evidence had been the same, I should have asked His Lordship with confidence to have withdrawn the case from you, and said the prosecution had absolutely broken down . . . because it is an absolutely indispensable part of the evidence of the prosecution to prove that the man charged with the murder did in fact kill and slay, and cause death; but, gentlemen, in this particular case, though from that aspect, Frederick, if I may put it so, is an innocent man, in another sense, by the operation of the principle of our law, he is brought within the four corners, of this charge of murder . . . Now just let us look for a moment at the evidence that bears upon the state of mind of Charles on that night. I venture to say that when we really consider the conversation and the behaviour of Charles on that night, you will come to the conclusion that he was not at any rate what may fairly be called a normal frame of mind. Men do not produce pistols and talk of 'Death or Glory' of sleeping in the fields, point to the temple, saying 'not tonight, in the morning' in everyday life. I have not the slightest doubt when you heard that bit of evidence as to pointing to the temple, if you had any doubt before, it absolutely removed from your minds any remaining doubt there might have been as to who at that moment, the intention of the unhappy man was; it was what one of the witnesses said he thought it was – the intention of self-destruction

His Lordship in his summing up, which commenced at 2.15 pm, said:

The question you have to decide is whether or not the prosecution have made out that Charles Benjamin Backhouse and Frederick Lawder Backhouse, or either of them, and if so which, is guilty of the murder of the policeman Kew. Now, of course, at the outset of the consideration of this case the fact appears that the fatal shot which killed the policeman was fired by Charles Benjamin Backhouse, whereas the shot which was fired by Frederick Lawder Backhouse did not kill, with whatever intent it was fired; therefore, you might, in the first instance suppose that there was a wide difference between the two cases; the one man's hand did the act by which the policeman met his death, the other man's hand did not. That is true, so far as it goes, but we have to apply the law to the facts in such a case, and what I have to tell you is this – and I think you will agree with me that the law in saying so is right – if two men go out together with a common design to murder a person, or if not deliberately to murder him, to use upon him a fatal weapon in such a way that it may cause his death, if they go out together with that common design, and then one of them, in the pursuance of that design, fires a fatal shot, the other who is there along with him at the same time is equally guilty. In the present instance, Frederick Lawder Backhouse, although he did not fire the shot which was fatal, he fired, as we have heard, another and subsequent shot, which would not by itself have caused the death of the policeman. The fact that he so fired is strong evidence upon which you might be asked to come to the conclusion that there was a common design between them, because if it were not so then, upon the firing of the first shot by Charles one would have expected Frederick, who by that supposition was no party to any common design, to have immediately resented it by his words and by his actions. In the present case he did neither; it therefore, would be a strong piece of evidence to show that he was there in pursuance of a common design, and, if so, if you thought the two were there together in pursuance of a common design, in pursuance of which the one of them fired the fatal shot, and the other consented to it, that ought to result in a verdict of murder against both men . . . Mr Mitchell Innes, who has defended the prisoners with very great ability, admits that he cannot contend before you that there was no common design between them. If he had not so admitted I can hardly help thinking you must have come to the conclusion that they were acting together. There is too much in the case to prove that they were so acting. That is to say, there is the fact that they were together throughout the evening, there is the fact that they kept together, that they used expressions, first one and then the other, indicating that both of them knew that a loaded revolver was in Charles's pocket; there is the action of each, the one fires and the other accepts the revolver from him and uses it again. There is also the fact, though I do not think it is so stringent or so important that both of them were in a way concerned in the matter of the summons which had been heard the day before . . .

The summing up lasted for thirty-six minutes and His Lordship concluded by saying:

> *. . . You have got to consider the evidence which bears for and against these men without flinching. Whatever you can find in their favour, which I may have omitted unconsciously in addressing you on this matter, you will please give it its full weight and place, from your own point of view, subject to what I have been able to tell you about the law in the matter. You will find your verdict on the facts as they bear against each prisoner separately; you will say if you find Charles or Frederick guilty or both of them. The matter is entirely in your hands subject to the observations I have made, and I am perfectly sure that in retiring to your room, as I have no doubt you will, you will carefully consider all the material that has been put before you, and not arrive at a conclusion without the full consideration which a case of this seriousness demands.*

The jury retired at 2.50 pm and returned as the Town Hall was striking four o'clock. After the usual formalities the Foreman of the jury said:

> *We find Charles Benjamin Backhouse guilty, and Frederick Lawder Backhouse guilty of aiding and abetting his brother. I am asked to mention a circumstance that has taken place. It was suggested . . .*

At this point His Lordship interrupted the Foreman and the following conversation took place:

His Lordship: *You had better let me ask you about that. You find Frederick Lawder Backhouse guilty of aiding and abetting. Do you find that he aided and abetted the firing of the shot in the crime, or that he consented to it after it was done, or that he aided and abetted in the sense that he was an accessory before the fact?*

Foreman: *That is the feeling of the jury, I believe.*

His Lordship: *I should like you to be sure. Do you find that he was a party to it before and at the time the act was committed?*

Foreman: *We do.*

His Lordship: *In consequence of what you have said have you any recommendation?*

Foreman: *It was suggested that we should recommend the younger prisoner to mercy, but on that point the jury did not agree.*

Kew Court, Piccadily, a modern development of houses named in memory of the slain policeman. The author

His Lordship: *I shall report that some of you wished to do so. For today that amounts to a verdict of guilty against both the prisoners.*

The Clerk of Arraigns then asked the prisoners if there was anything they wished to say why judgement should not be passed upon them according to the law. There was an uncomfortable pause which lasted several seconds, during which neither of the prisoners spoke. They appeared to be somewhat dazed and unable to comprehend the seriousness of their situation. His Lordship having put on the black cap then passed sentence of death on both prisoners and the prisoners were led from the dock.

Both the Backhouse brothers were kept at Armley Gaol, where on 1 August Charles wrote a letter to his wife:

Her Majesty's Prison, Leeds   *August 1st 1900*

Dear wife,
I now take the pleasure in answering your letter. You know I like to hear from my dear old home. Dear Gertie they won't let me send a letter to put in the newspaper, so you will have to bear it. You know, dear, your troubles are not half so bad as mine are to bear, but I keep up my

heart. Just fancy knowing this day you are going to die; it would seem hard to bear. Never mind what people say about me; I am suffering for what I have done. It is hard to sit in a prison cell all day and night, thinking of home and of you and my dear little angel; but, dear you will promise me you will take care of our Ethel for the one who is in Heaven. Tell your father to give over with that drink, or he will rue it. It is drink that has brought me here, for I know no more about shooting Mr Kew than our Ethel knows. I had never the thought on my mind of doing such a thing, for I always was fond of Mr Kew. The chaplain comes to me every morning, and prays for me, and every morning and evening I pray for myself and for you and my little angel. I pray the Lord to lead you

Charles Backhouse signs his will in the condemned cell at Armley Gaol, Leeds. Giles Brearley Collection

on the right path, so dear, I am well prepared to die. The Lord will forgive me for what I have done. I suppose our Maggie and Chrissie will be down hearted, but tell them not to bother about us. I cannot see our Fred, so I do not know what he has to say. If I was you I should leave Piccadilly. If the people won't let you alone you know you can go to my mother's and stay there; then you will be out of the way of everybody, but please yourself what you do, but whatever you do, do it honest. Write back soon; tell me all the news. What is the reason that Jack has gone home? I suppose he is ashamed of himself for what he has told about me. He said that I was sober. He knows it is a lie, for I had been drinking all day, and the week before. When he was at the Town Hall he could not look at me in the face, nor his mate, Gibbins, either; but tell them from me, it will all come home to them before so long. There was not one that could look us in the face only your Harriet, and I felt sorry for her; for if it had been left to Harriet we should not have been hanged, but she was forced to say what she had seen. Perhaps you do not know what I mean. When I got your letter this morning, and was reading it, tears rolled down my face like peas. I had three or four tries before I could read it through. You must excuse this letter, because you know I have a poor hand at making a letter up. You know, dear, every letter that comes here or goes away is read, and the Governor says I am not allowed to send a letter for the papers, or else I would do for the sake of you and our Ethel. It is getting dark now, and I cannot see to write. I will write again soon. If I were you I should not come on Monday; come later on, because it will be the LAST time I shall see you; so no more this time. Tell all my friends that I send my best love, and accept the same yourself, and kiss our little Ethel for me. Good-day and God bless you all. Give my best love to your father.

At the foot of the letter are eleven crosses representing kisses. A little over a week later another letter to Gertie Backhouse followed:

Her Majesty's Prison, Leeds   *August 9th 1900*

Dear Wife,
I now take the pleasure of answering your kind and loving letter. You will think I was never going to write to you. I am pleased to hear that you are making your home with your Annie. I know you will be all right there. If you wish to write a letter to our Fred you may do so. You must put him a letter inside of mine, and they will give it to him. I feel sorry for him, poor lad. Dear Gertie, if you are coming to see me I should not come before Monday or Tuesday; you know the time is rolling on now. I have only a week today to live (Thursday), so I have not long to stay in this world. Tell your father I shall be very pleased to see him. You know I was always fond of your father, and tell my friends who would like to come I should be very glad to see them all. Dear Gertie, you must not forget to bring our little Ethel; you know it is a long time since I saw her. She will not know me when she comes. God bless her! Our little Thomas will never know the wrong I have done. I have not forgotten him if I am in a prison cell. I have not been the same man since he died, but I know he is in heaven, so my mind is at rest. I often think about him when he asked me the night before he died for some milk. Those were the last words. When you write again tell me what is the matter at home. I think there is something wrong, for I have never had a letter or seen them since we came from Rotherham. I do not know their address so I cannot write to them. Tell me the truth if my mother is ill or not. I think all my friends and relatives have forgotten we are here. I know it runs away with a lot of money, but if it was me I should see them no matter what it cost. Dear Gertie, have you heard

anything from Hood Hill, or any other of my relations? If so write and tell me. Tell our Maggie and Chrissie to put a line or two in your letter. You never say how they are getting on. I don't know whether they are dead or not. Did you tell your father what I had told you to. Do tell Mr Machen I often think about what he said to me about taming a lion. Here they can tame two lions, but you know they are very good to me. Dear Gertie, when you go to Maud and Ada's tell them all I send my best respects to them. You know I am not in the cell myself; there are two men with me night and day. So I think this is all this time. Give our Ethel a kiss for me. Write back soon; don't forget. From your husband C. Backhouse

Again this letter concludes with a series of crosses for kisses.
The younger brother had also written a number of letters:

Her Majesty's Prison, Leeds

Dear Harry,

I write these few lines hoping to find you quite well, as it leaves me at present. Dear Harry, you would be surprised to hear about this affair, but it was done in drink. You can come and see me if you wish it, and tell Herbert and Harry I should like to see them. Dear Harry, you must come if you can get. If you come you will have to call at the Leeds Town Hall, and get an order from the chairman of the Visiting Committee, through Mr Thornton, before you can see me. I wish I was having another spin with you old boy. I think this is all this time, from your loving friend

Fred Backhouse

Give my best love to all my old pals, so good-day and God bless you. Write back old boy.

Another letter read:

Her Majesty's Prison, Leeds   *10th August 1900*

Dear Harry,

I thank you very much for your letter. You will understand that in this position a kind friendly letter comes as a great pleasure to me. I am pleased to tell you that my position is made as light as possible, and everything is done for me to add to my comfort. I shall indeed be very pleased to have a visit from you; nothing would please me better; but you must not come on Sunday, visits not being allowed on that day. Tomorrow, Saturday, will be suitable if it is convenient for you. Before you come to the prison call at the Leeds Town Hall, and get an order from Mr Thornton, the magistrates' clerk, to see me. Be sure to be at the prison before four o'clock, as visitors are not allowed after that time. Hoping to see you very shortly, I will now remain, with kindest regards,

your old friend
Frank Backhouse

The three young men referred to in the above letter came to visit Frank Backhouse on Monday. They were workmates of his at Thrybergh Hall Colliery. Henry Beighton and Herbert Law, were from Kilnhurst. The other, Henry Lawcook, came from Sandhill, Rawmarsh. Although the three men had difficulty obtaining the necessary warrant to see Frederick Backhouse, when they showed him the letters and explained the distance they had travelled, Mr Thornton gave his consent and they were allowed a twenty minute visit.

On the following day, Tuesday 14 August, the Governor at Armley Gaol, received an intimation that Her Majesty had been graciously pleased to give effect to the recommendation of mercy, and that in the case of the younger brother a reprieve was granted.

When Charles Backhouse received the news of his brother's reprieve he registered a look of tremendous satisfaction. On Friday 17 August 1900, the *Mexborough and Swinton Times* reported on the execution which had taken place on the previous day. Part of the article reads:

Charles Backhouse has all along shown the most repentant spirit. He was quite resigned to his fate, and according to his own statement, Wednesday was the happiest day he had spent since his conviction, and he expressed himself ready and anxious for the end to come. The news of the reprieve of his younger brother, Fredrick Lauder Back-house, was received by him on Tuesday with great joy, though he naturally expressed some regret that the clemency of the Crown had not been extended to himself.

Charles Backhouse was hanged in the company of one other murderer, Tom Mellor, sentenced for child murder at Holbrook. Mellor was a former resident of Swinton and had relatives living both in Swinton and in Mexborough. The report went on:

The condemned men passed a fairly good night, and were awakened shortly after six o'clock yesterday morning. At half past seven breakfast was provided them, and both made a fairly good meal. They seemed thoroughly resigned to their fate, and offered no opposition when the executioner entered and pinioned them. They walked to the scaffold, each between two warders, with a firm step, and seemed to pay great attention to the burial service repeated by the Prison Chaplain.

The proceedings were witnessed by the Under Sheriff of Yorkshire, Edward Grey, Esquire, the Governor of the gaol, John Henry Shepherd, Esquire, the Deputy Medical Officer, Dr J Exley, and the Chaplain, the Rev H M Thompson. An hour later the bodies were cut down and placed in two of the prison cells. At half past ten, J C Malcomb, Esquire, the Leeds City coroner, opened the inquest. The coroner, addressing the jury, said:

These proceedings though somewhat formal are necessary under provision of the Capital Punishment Act. You must satisfy yourselves as representing the public as to the identity of the bodies you will view, and satisfy yourselves also that the sentence of death which was passed upon them has been duly executed.

The proceedings were then adjourned while the jury went to view the bodies. That task being done, the inquest was then

The execution of Charles Backhouse. Giles Brearley Collection

The grave of PC William Kew, in the churchyard of St Margaret's Church, Swinton.
The author

resumed. James Henry Shepherd, Esquire, governor at Armley, in his evidence stated that with regards to the body of Charles Benjamin Backhouse, he was received at Wakefield Prison and transferred to Armley Gaol, where he remained in his custody until that morning when he was handed over to the custody of the Under Sheriff, and sentence of death was carried out in both his own and the Under Sheriff's presence.

Dr John Exley, the Deputy Medical Officer at Armley Gaol, said:

> *I was present this morning when the sentence of death was carried out on Charles Benjamin Backhouse and death was due to dislocation of the vertebra by hanging . . . death was instantaneous.*

In the case of both hanged men the jury returned a verdict to the effect that in both cases the sentence had been duly carried out.

CHAPTER 9

Barnsley Love Tragedy Ends in Suicide
1903

This unfortunate woman seemingly almost in protection of herself appears to have taken her life.

On Saturday 25 July 1903, the body of a young woman was pulled from the canal at Barnsley by miner, Arthur Watson, of Smithies Lane. On Monday 27 July, an inquest was held at the *New Inn*, Gawber on the body of twenty-one-year-old Charlotte Porrill, daughter of a carter, John Porrill, of 15 Brinckman Street, Barnsley, before the District Coroner, P P Maitland, Esquire. A jury was chosen and Richard Binns was elected foreman.

Evidence of identification was given by the deceased woman's sister, Theresa Porrill. She said her sister was a tailoress at Mr Cass's establishment in Barnsley, and was last at work on Friday week. Although she had received no medical attention Miss Porrill had been complaining about pains in her head for several weeks. She had also had some trouble with a young man who worked at the same establishment as herself, named John Naylor, who worked as the cutter out:

Coroner: *You say she had trouble: well what is it?*

Miss Porrill: *Well, you see, he's married, and it seems he has been wanting to take her away. He told her that he loved her. She had not wanted to go, and he has written several letters to her.*

Coroner: *Did you see them?*

Miss Porrill: *Well, I did not see them, but she read them to me.*

Coroner: *How long has this been going on?*

Miss Porrill: *About eight months.*

Coroner: *She knew he was married?*

Miss Porrill: *Yes; and she wanted to avoid him.*

Coroner: *They would meet at work most days?*

Miss Porrill: *Yes.*

Coroner: *And has he been in the habit of taking her out in the evening for walks?*

Miss Porrill: *I don't think they have been out for walks, but they have met.*

Coroner: *They have met near your house?*

Mis Porrill: *Well, not far from where we live.*

Coroner: Have you seen them together?

Miss Porrill: No. I have not seen them.

Coroner: But she has told you of it?

Miss Porrill: Yes. She has told me.

Coroner: But as they met every day, I was wondering why did he write to her? Has he written to her through the post?

Miss Porrill: *No, he has written the letters and given them to her as she passed up and down the warehouse.*

Coroner: *Several letters?*

Miss Porrill: Yes.

Coroner: *Did she write to him?*

Miss Porrill: *I think she wrote two letters, but I think he destroyed them because she told him to.*

Coroner: *And she read all those letters to you in your bedroom?*

Miss Porrill: *Yes.*

Coroner; *Was there any request, or did he suggest that she should go away with him?*

Miss Porrill: *He wanted her to go, but he said he would not compel her, not without she wanted to go of her own free will.*

Coroner: *Did he want to go away, or send her away?*

Miss Porrill: *He wanted to go with her.*

Miss Porrill: *Did he suggest any place?*

Miss Porrill: *No.*

Coroner: *Was that stated in the letters?*

Miss Porrill: *No; it was not in the letters, but he had told her.*

Coroner: *What were the letters about?*

Miss Porrill: *They were mostly about love, nothing else.*

Coroner: *Love-making?*

Miss Porrill: *Yes.*

Coroner; *When he was asking her to go away, did she tell you she had refused?*

Miss Porrill: *Yes.*

Coroner: *More than once?*

Miss Porrill: *Yes, several times she had refused.*

Coroner: *Then had there been any dispute between them or any quarrel?*

Miss Porrill: *I don't know as there had been a quarrel, only he has been rather jealous of her, and he has had a few words to say to her, now and again.*

Miss Porrill was shown a bundle of letters, which were found in the deceased's possession when the body was recovered. They were written in pencil and Miss Porrill confirmed they were like those she had seen. The writing was faint and with some difficulty Police Sergeant Whiteley was able to read the greater part of the contents:

My Own Sweetheart,

Why did you not come down yesterday afternoon? Why did you play such a devil's trick? It was one of the most cruel tricks you could have played on me. Are you trying to drive me to destruction and the devil, or what are you trying to do knowing that you would not seem me coming home, and not to come near all the afternoon. I was by myself. It was heartlessly cruel. You know how I love you my darling. Do for the love of God show a little love in return. I expect I shall not be able to see you again this week by yourself. You can't say you had not to come down for anything, for you came down twice for things you could have come for to me. It has been the most miserable half-day and night I have spent in my life, and I hope I shall not spend another like it. If you don't change Lancet [Langsett] for somewhere else I shall say you have gone there because Clayton has gone. Don't go, love, for my sake. I love you from the crown of my dear head to the soles of your feet. Be true to your own true, loving Jack.

The coroner: *Did she read that to you?*

Miss Porrill: *Yes, but it is several weeks ago.*

Miss Porrill added that her sister knew a man by the name of Clayton but she did not go with him. Another letter read as follows:

Dear Charlotte,

Now, how do you like that for a start? Yours was 'Dear Jack' first, 'Dear John' next time; I expect it will be 'Mr. Naylor'. It was very good of you, love, to come down for something yesterday afternoon, but I expect you had not time to spare for me, as usual. Never mind it. It will please you to know it hurt me more than your letter. I call it a bone thrown at a barking dog. I don't want a bone; I want a letter from the very centre; I want a little from the heart. – Your faithful and loving sweetheart.

At this point Sergeant Whiteley mentioned that the letters bore no dates and that they had crosses at the end of every line or two. Most of them were signed 'J.W.N.'

Coroner: *Has he said anything in any of the letters about going away with him?*

Officer: *No sir; I don't think so.*

Miss Porrill: *He asked her to go away, but she told him he had a wife and two children; and that he ought to look after them. She did not want to go away with him. I believe the last time Charlotte saw Naylor was on Thursday night, when she met him under the railway bridge at the Barnsley Station, and he brought her to the top of Brinckman Street.*

Coroner: *They did not quarrel?*

Miss Porrill: *She did not say anything, but on Friday I asked her what was the matter with her she was so quiet.*

Coroner: *When was that?*

Miss Porrill: *In the evening.*

Coroner: *What did she say?*

Miss Porrill: *I asked her three times but she said nothing.*

Coroner: *She seemed depressed?*

Miss Porrill: *She was depressed and tired, because she had been helping mother to wash, a thing she seldom does.*

Coroner: *Did she go to be on Friday night?*

Miss Porrill: *Yes, she went upstairs in the evening, and threw herself on the bed. When I got upstairs at eleven o'clock she was just undressing.*

Coroner: *Did she get up during the night?*

Miss Porrill: *She must have done, but we did not hear her.*

Miss Porrill said she woke up on Saturday morning at seven o'clock. Her sister, Charlotte, had by then gone out and she was under the misapprehension that Charlotte was lighting the fire, which she habitually did. Charlotte had not in fact lit the fire, and everybody in the household thought she had gone to work. She did not come home to dinner but her absence did not arouse any suspicion because it was usual for her to spend the day with a particular friend. Miss Porrill said that about seven in the evening she began to feel a little uneasy, and was just about to set out in search of her sister, when a policeman called to say her body had been found in the canal.

> Coroner: *Did neither your mother nor your father know about your sister's relationship with this man Naylor?*
> Miss Porrill: *No, she wanted me to keep it secret, as she was going to keep it a secret, and I did so.*
> Coroner: *Had she any other sweetheart?*
> Miss Porrill: *Well, she had at first, but she gave him up.*

Another letter was then read out:

> *My Dearest Darling,*
> *You little know how happy you made me when you gave me that note yesterday. Thank you, my love, for it. I am very sorry I made you miserable, love; for I want you to be happy, and I thought if I was out of the way you could do just as you pleased without being told about it. Can you suggest any other way, for I can't bear to keep being told about you standing talking to men. Have you no women friends? I have seen you speak to many men, but I have not seen you speak to one woman yet. If it is Mary that wants to stop and speak to them, she is altogether a different sort of girl I took her for, and I should give her up and find another companion. Surely, love you can find a good true woman friend. I want you to give up your old life entirely, and begin a new one. If you want to go to a place of worship go to ours; I think it is the nearest to your house, you can't find a better place. They're all so homelike, and there is not a better minister in Barnsley than ours. Think, dear heart, and try. For I can't bear the other . . . I fully intend doing what I told you, for I was tired of life. I prayed about it, and I see no other way, for I love you more than life. You know that it is for yourself that I love you, and not for what I could get. Do think, sweet-heart, and try to lead a new life. You will be happier then. I will do anything for you, love. I shall have to give up now, as the lodger is getting up. Write again, darling, and tell me your love and everything. Don't be in a hurry the next time. From your own true faithful and loving sweetheart. J. W. N.*

The dialogue continued:

> Coroner: *Did she tell you he had threatened to drown himself?*
> Miss Porrill: *He had threatened his life. He wanted her to write to him, but she refused. She didn't want to write. When she read that letter she cried bitterly and wrote to him.*

Coroner: *I suppose she was really attached to him? Was she fond of him?*

Miss Porrill: *She didn't use to be, but I think he has fair forced it out of her. She never encouraged him in any way.*

Another note was read out:

If you love me write; if you do not return me the notes, and you shall have the last one for a keepsake.

Miss Porrill said that note had been received about eight weeks previously.

Coroner: *Has she not had any this last week or two?*
Miss Porrill: *It is about three weeks ago since she had one.*
Coroner: *Did she ever in your presence threaten suicide?*
Miss Porrill: *No.*

The second witness to be called was John William Naylor, tailor's cutter, of Ouselthwaite Cottage, near Barnsley. Mr Naylor said he had known the deceased since he had come to Barnsley the previous October:

Coroner: *Have you been keeping company with her?*
J W N: *Partly.*
Coroner: *What do you mean by that?*
J W N: *I have gone backwards and forwards from my work with her.*
Coroner: *When did you see her last?*
J W N: *About half-past two on Friday afternoon.*
Coroner: *Was there anything special on Friday afternoon?*
J W N: *Yes, she said the girls in the shop had been scolding at her.*
Coroner: *For going with you?*
J W N: *On Thursday night I saw her near the station and walked with her to the street where she lives. I left her there and continued my way home. During that time one of the girls in the shop saw us, and on Friday it had gone round the shop and the girls made it so hot that it was almost past bearing. It was also said we had been seen in the park but this was a lie.*
Coroner: *And you say she was depressed?*
J W N: *I should say she was cut up.*
Coroner: *Are you a married man?*
J W N: *Yes.*
Coroner: *With a family?*
J W N: *Yes.*

Coroner: *Are you not ashamed of yourself?*

J W N: *I am thoroughly. I deserve all that is possible.*

Coroner: *It is a most wicked thing. This poor girl's life has been lost, and according to the evidence which I have taken so far it was not a case of mutual affection, but you have persuaded and cajoled until she has been absolutely forced to go on with you.*

J W N: *I don't know about forced.*

Coroner: *I am stating to you what has been given in evidence. I don't know what the jury will say about it, but your conduct in this matter, so far as I can judge at present has been infamous.*

At this point the foreman of the jury said I think that you, a married man, with two children, ought to have had more sense:

Coroner: *It is disgraceful.*

Foreman: *What made you do so? What made you make company with that girl?*

J W N: *Well at the first, in the beginning, it was purely friendship.*

Foreman: *It's very poor friendship.*

Coroner: *I think that is sufficient.*

The next witness called was Arthur Watson, who found the body; and who said he first saw a hat lying on the bridge and letters were floating on the water. The deceased woman was in the water near to the canal bank, and she appeared to have walked into the water. In her hand she held a Sankey hymn book and some of the letters, written by Naylor. The coroner said there seemed little doubt that his young woman had committed suicide, and the conduct of Naylor was highly censurable. This unfortunate woman seemingly almost in protection of herself appears to have taken her life. The man's conduct was not actually criminal, but morally there were no words strong enough for his conduct. It is a most pathetic affair. The jury returned a verdict of 'Committed suicide whilst of unsound mind' and expressed sympathy with the deceased's family. Naylor was brought back into the room. The coroner told him that the jury were of the opinion that the woman had drowned herself whilst temporarily insane, through his persecuting manner of paying addresses to her. He had really driven her to the suicide and it was a lasting shame to him. The jury considered he was to blame to a great extent in endeavouring to persuade her to go away with him when he had a wife and family.

CHAPTER 10

The Chinese Laundry Murder in Sheffield
1922

I not know, I think he go back to China. This business belong to me now.

Sing Lee was already the successful owner of a Chinese Laundry in Liverpool, when in 1919 he opened his second such establishment at 231 Crookes Road, Sheffield. The building was a seven-roomed house with shop premises on the ground floor fronting the street. This new business proved popular and grew from strength to strength. By the summer of 1922, as well as various laundry staff, the shop also employed twenty-seven-year-old Lee Doon (also known as Leong Lun) and the shop manager, twenty-three-year-old Lily Siddall, who lived with her parents at 154 Forncett Street, Sheffield. The shop's owner, Sing Lee, had by this time become a familiar figure in the neighbourhood. He was highly regarded for his scrupulous honesty and his shop was noted for its particular cleanliness. Sheffield's small Chinese community looked up to Sing Lee as a man they could turn to should the need arise.

On Saturday 9 September 1922, the shop was particularly busy. Miss Siddall did not leave the premises until 8.30 pm and as she said goodnight to Sing Lee, she left him in the company of Lee Doon. When she arrived at 11.30 am on

Sing Lee. Press Archive

Sunday morning to open the shop, she was confronted by Lee Doon who was already up and about, which was not the usual occurrence, as both Sing Lee and Lee Doon generally slept in on a Sunday in the living quarters upstairs. When Sing Lee did not make his customary appearance Miss Siddall asked Lee Doon where he was. The answer which he gave to her question startled Miss Siddall, to say the least, because when she asked where Sing Lee was, Lee Doon replied that he had gone away. Eager to know more, Miss Siddall pressed Lee Doon further. She asked him where he had gone, then came the ominous reply:

I not know, I think he go back to China. This business belong to me now.

Miss Siddall was not impressed by Lee Doon's explanation and thought it was a little odd. She had worked at the laundry since February and got on very well with Sing Lee, and found it difficult to believe that he would disappear like that without saying anything.

When Miss Siddall turned up for work on the following day she heard the sound of digging in the cellar. She enquired of Lee Doon if the landlord had sent some workmen but he told her it was none of her business. However, Miss Siddall's curiosity got the better of her and she was determined to find out exactly what was going on, so she went down into the cellar. There she was confronted by two men with picks and shovels. When she asked what they were doing she was told that Lee Doon had approached them on Sunday and told them he wanted a hole digging in the cellar, so that is what they were doing. Later in the day Lee Doon went out, so in his absence Miss Siddall decided that a spot of amateur detective work was the order of the day. She went into the living quarters and entered Sing Lee's bedroom. In it, as well as his hat and attaché case, there were several other articles, which Sing Lee habitually took with him when he went away on business. How very curious, she thought. Miss Siddall then went back downstairs and carried on with her normal duties.

When Miss Siddall arrived at the shop on Tuesday Lee Doon told her that someone had fetched Sing Lee's trunk and taken it away in a taxi. As Lee Doon was telling Miss Siddall this latest piece of news, he was wearing a pair of Sing Lee's trousers. When asked why he was wearing them he said his own were dirty and were being washed. She also asked him why he was washing Sing

Sing Lee's Chinese Laundry, at 231 Crookes Road. Press Archive

Lee's bedding and why there was blood on one of the windows. Lee Doon replied:

Bedding dirty. Blood from chicken.

That afternoon two parcels arrived, addressed to Lee Doon. Judging by the contents it would appear that Lee Doon had decided to adopt a more proprietorial role, for the parcels contained a new hat and a shiny new pair of shoes. Later that afternoon Lee Doon overstepped the mark with Miss Siddal by making a lascivious remark, which she greatly resented, and she showed her displeasure by pushing him away. Having offered her 30s to look after the shop for the rest of the week, she told him to look after it himself. On Wednesday morning she went back to the shop and asked if there had been any communication from Sing Lee. When Lee Doon replied in the negative, Miss Siddall told him she would not be coming back to work until Sing Lee returned.

Thomas Marshall, living at 7 Toftwood Road, Crookes, was a particular friend of Sing Lee. On the Friday before Sing Lee's disappearance the two friends had made a tentative arrangement to go to the Hippodrome on Monday. When Mr Marshall called into the shop on Monday and enquired of Lee Doon about his friend's whereabouts he was told that a telegram had arrived and Sing Lee had gone to London taking £100 with him. Puzzled by this Mr Marshall returned to the shop later that evening. The shop door was locked but through the window he saw Lee Doon struggling with a trunk.

Miss Siddall continued to call in at the shop to see if there was any news of Sing Lee. She sent off a telegram to the shop in Prescott Road, Liverpool, to ask if Sing Lee had paid them a visit. A telegram came back saying that he had not visited them. On the Thursday, four days after Sing Lee's disappearance, Miss Siddall once again called in at the shop to enquire about Sing Lee. Lee Doon said:

Don't think boss come back any more. Perhaps go to China. Perhaps go to Liverpool.

Miss Siddal called on Sing Sai, a friend of Sing Lee, who lived in Barnsley Road, Crookes. By now she was deeply concerned and decided to go to Liverpool. There she spoke to Sing Lee's cousin, Sun Kwong Lee. She told him all that had occurred since the previous Sunday and he agreed to accompany her back to Sheffield. Shortly after their arrival in the early hours of Saturday morning they went immediately to the police. It was not long before a contingent of police had been dispatched to Crookes and they were soon at the laundry knocking on the shop door. When Lee Doon answered the door he was asked the whereabouts of Sing Lee, to which he replied they had gone away. An inspection of the cellar was requested.

The cellar was well stocked with coal and coke and in all appearances everything seemed to be perfectly in order. It was only after some of the coal and coke had been removed that the obvious signs of recent digging became evident, as signs of the clay floor's disturbance was revealed. It was approaching daybreak when the officers began digging. Lee Doon remained perfectly calm and said nothing. It was not long before a shovel struck something hard and the clank of metal was heard. A metal trunk was soon revealed and this was dug out and carried upstairs. The trunk had a domed lid. It was 29½ inches long by 18 inches wide and 22 inches high. When it was opened it contained the body of Sing Lee. Lee Doon was immediately placed under arrest and removed from the premises. He said he didn't understand what was happening. When searched he was found to have £30 on him and he was also wearing a ring belonging to Sing Lee. It was established that two of the £5 notes contained within the £30 found on Lee Doon's person had been paid to Sing Lee during the week before his disappearance.

Police Surgeon and University Lecturer in Forensic Medicine, Dr Carter, arrived at the scene and examined the trunk and its contents. Sing Lee's body was lying on its back, tied with a rope, with its knees flexed and a running noose round the neck. The body was dressed in only singlet and drawers. There were gaping wounds to the head, one wound which was very deep, extended from the ear to beneath the jaw. Inside the trunk were a blood-stained pillow and pillow case

The post-mortem examination revealed there were extensive fractures of the skull, including severe fractures at the base of the skull on the left side. The stomach contents revealed that the deceased had eaten a meal of rice and lentils about an hour and a half before he had died. The injuries, which could not have been self-inflicted, had been caused by a blunt instrument. The bloodstained pillow and pillow case were indicative that Sing Lee had been killed in bed. The cause of death was head injuries and haemorrhage.

Lee Doon was brought before Sheffield city magistrates at 10.30 am that morning. When asked if he understood English, the smartly dressed Chinaman shook his head. Lee Doon was remanded in custody until the following Friday. On Monday 18 September, Coroner J Kenyon Parker, Esquire, opened the inquest at the Nursery Street Coroner's Court. Language difficulties among witnesses resulted in an adjournment until 2.30 pm on Friday. Sing Lee's funeral took place on Thursday 20 September. He was buried in a section of Anfield Cemetery, Liverpool, reserved for Chinese burials.

The resumed inquest took place the following day. Miss Siddall, Dr Carter and the officers who discovered the trunk gave their evidence and when Lee Doon was asked if he wished to give evidence – to the surprise of all concerned – he replied that he did. Despite having said before the magistrates that he didn't understand English, Lee Doon proved to have a good command of the language. He said:

> *Sing Lee wrote to me in Manchester and asked me to come to Sheffield. I saw him taking morphia and I told him not to do it and he started fighting with me. We had a fight and I struck him. I found I had killed him. At the time I did not know the consequence. I was afraid and put him in the box. Then I took the box down to the cellar. I then engaged two men to dig a hole so that I could hide it and no one would be any the wiser. I covered the hole up . . .*

The coroner's jury returned a verdict of wilful murder. On the following day Lee Doon was once again before the city magistrates. Sydney Robinson, Esquire and J W Flint, Esquire, appeared for the Director of Public Prosecutions and Sheffield solicitor appeared for Lee Doon. Mr Flint commended Miss Siddall for her detective work. When asked if he wished to make a statement, Lee Doon said he wished to reserve his defence. He was committed to take his trial at the Assizes.

Lee Doon was tried before Mr Justice Greer at Leeds Winter Gaol Delivery, on 1 December 1922. Mr W J Waugh KC, with Mr H V Rabaghati, appeared for the prosecution and Mr W P Donald, for the defence. The main thrust of the case for the prosecution was that even if the two men quarrelled, the amount of force used to inflict the injuries went far beyond anything necessary for Lee Doon's own defence; and the evidence of Dr Carter, the police surgeon, that Sing Lee had been killed in his bed seemed to negate any other claim. When Lee Doon went into the witness box, he said:

> *On the Sunday after closing the shop at 9.00 pm I went into the drying room at the back of the house and lay on a sofa there. Sing Lee, after removing the silver from the till upstairs, came into the drying room and stood in front of the stove. He said 'I wish I had an opium pipe so that I coulod have a smoke. It would be worth 3s to have a smoke.' I asked him what he wanted to smoke opium for. I said 'You have only £300 or £400 saved up and, if they get to know, you will be arrested. Lee replied his smoking had nothing to do with him. He got vexed and made use of abusive language. I retorted by calling him a few names. He rolled up his sleeves and said he wanted to fight. He came for me and then there was a fight and in the fight we fell to the ground, Lee striking his head on the stove. A flat iron fell from the stove and hit Lee*

on the head. Lee said that I was illegitimate and had no ancestors and it made me very angry. When I saw Lee was bleeding I wrapped his head up in two towels and took him back upstairs and put him on the bed. I put two pillows under him to raise him up, took his shirt and trousers off and covered him up with a blanket. I went for a drink for him and on my return I found him dead. I got frightened, saw the trunk and put him in it. He was too long for the trunk so I put one rope round his neck and the other round his feet to pull him together so that he would fit into the box. He had then been dead an hour. I got frightened. I knew I should be held responsible for his death so I thought I would bury him. I washed up the blood.

Under cross-examination, the prisoner admitted he had battered Sing Lee's head against the flat iron five or six times. Lee Doon then said:

I took him by the armpits to get him upstairs. At that stage he had the use of his legs.

Dr Carter was recalled at this point and gave the opinion that he did not believe that Sing Lee would have been conscious after being struck with the iron and could not have taken any part in going up the stairs. In his closing speech for the defence Mr Donald contented that the blows the accused struck were in self defence and that, it was not proved that when he struck them he intended either to kill or to cause grievous bodily harm to Sing Lee.

Mr Justice Greer, in his summing up, drew the jury's attention to the contradictory nature of Lee Doon's evidence. The jury returned a verdict of guilty and His Lordship duly donned the customary black cap and passed sentence of death. Lee Doon was hanged at Armley Gaol on 5 January 1923 by Thomas Pierrepoint.

CHAPTER 11

The Wombwell Stabbing Affray
1925

I says in my own mind, 'Tha will have to shake thysen up a bit Amos. It looks like being a bit hot.'

John William Jones, a miner aged fifty-five-year-old, of 23 Elliott's Terrace, Wombwell, pleaded not guilty to the charge of the wilful murder, on 8 February, of thirty-five-year-old miner Walter Taylor, of Station Lane, Wombwell, when he appeared before Mr Justice Branson, in the Crown Court at Leeds Assizes, on Monday 23 March 1923.

Mr H Brent Grotrain, KC, when opening the case for the prosecution, referred to the evidence proffered at Barnsley West Riding Court, during the committal proceedings, said, on the day previous to the tragedy, 7 April, there had been some quarrelling. Mr Grotrain said he was not suggesting that the prisoner had anything to do with those quarrels, nor that he had any quarrel with the deceased man. On 8 April, the prisoner and his son, Tom, went to Joseph Dyson's house in Station Lane, Wombwell, at about two thirty in the afternoon. The prisoner said to Joseph Dyson, 'What about this bother Joe,' and Dyson replied, 'I know nothing about it.' Prisoner replied, 'It looks like murder then.' They left the house and the prisoner remarked, 'Someone is going to get it.' They went into Station Lane, and there they saw prisoner's son, George Jones, and Edward Taylor, a brother of the deceased man, fighting. Walter Taylor was there, and to him the prisoner said, 'Let them fight – let them fight – let them have it out.' Walter Taylor, it was stated, replied, 'To hell with that,' attempting at the same time to separate the combatants. Whereupon, according to the evidence, the prisoner went to Walter

Taylor and stabbed him twice in the back with a dagger, behind the shoulder blade, and Taylor collapsed on the ground, and died.

The next day Dr Foley made a post-mortem examination of the body and found Taylor had two wounds behind the right shoulder blade. They had penetrated three inches deep through the chest wall, and had also penetrated the lung. Dr Foley expressed the opinion that considerable force must have been used.

Mr Grotrain said if it were suggested that general fighting was going on, and that the prisoner joined in, he would not answer that fighting of that sort did not justify a man taking a knife and stabbing another in the back.

Samuel Bowen, miner, of 64 Station Road, Wombwell, confirmed Mr Grotrain's statement and added that he saw the prisoner strike one blow. During the course of a long cross-examination by Mr Donald, the witness said there was a lot of 'scrapping' going on. All the parties were, in general, friendly with one another, but a quarrel had arisen in the *Station Hotel* the night before. Harry Jones, a son of the prisoner, missed a 10*s* note, and it was hinted that Edward Dyson had taken it. Later, Jones found the note in his waistcoat pocket. He apologized and asked all those present to have a drink. Edward Dyson not only refused to have a drink but also to shake hands.

After eighteen witnesses had been called for the defence, Mr H B Grotrain, KC, for the prosecution, said he could not ask the jury to find the prisoner guilty of murder, but he would press very strongly for a verdict of manslaughter. He said he realised there was great provocation, so he was willing to withdraw the charge of murder, and he understood that in the circumstances the defence would plead guilty to the charge of manslaughter.

In reply to counsel's suggestion that the prisoner's visit to Dyson's house on Sunday afternoon was with the object of settling matters amicably, Mr Bowen would not agree that it was. He thought John William Jones had come to match one of his sons against one of Joe Dyson's sons with the ideas of settling the dispute that way.

John Lingard, who struggled with the prisoner, said he observed what appeared to be a second knife in Jones's other hand.

Edward Dyson, aged fifty-four, of Station Lane, Wombwell, said he saw the prisoner strike Taylor twice with some instrument. He denied in cross-examination that one of the Jonses had agreed to fight him on condition that he took his boots off. It was not a habit of his to kick. Mr Donald suggested that the witness had got several men to join in the fight, and then, like a prudent general, let the men go on while he went round the different groups kicking the men. Among others, he kicked the prisoner. Dyson denied these allegations.

Joseph Dyson, miner, of 70 Station Lane, Wombwell, said that as far as he knew there was no ill-feeling between Jones and Walter Taylor. They had been neighbours and friends. On the Sunday when the fight took place he saw Mark Jones had a hammer.

Alfred Lingard said that Amos Jones struck him over the nose with a hammer and then on the head. He himself was on a 'peace-making job', not out for a fight. Ellis Lingard , brother of the last witness, said that he saw the prisoner coming out of Dyson's house. Walking behind him, he exchanged a few words with the prisoner, who struck him on the back. He felt blood trickling down his back, and found that he had been stabbed, his wound being about the depth of a finger. He found a large rasp shortly after-wards and threw it into the garden.

For the defence, Mr Donald submitted that the killing was done because Jones imagined that his son's life was in danger, and, at most, it was no more than manslaughter. The object of the prisoner's visit to Dyson's house was to make peace, and inde-pendent witnesses would say that the interference of the deceased, was not with the object of stopping the fight between young Jones and Edward Taylor, but for the purpose of joining in it. The father believed his son was being strangled, and took the unfortunate course he did.

The prisoner, in his evidence, said there was no ill-feeling between himself and the dead man at the time of the tragedy. After hearing the accounts of the trouble shortly before, he, with his son, Tom, went to see Dyson, because he thought Dyson was the man who could stop it. The prisoner's son, Harry, and Bowen were the first to start fighting. Jones went on to say that his son appealed to him for aid and he had tried to separate them. As he went further on, he saw his son, Amos, lying on the ground covered with blood and surrounded by several others. It was the prisoner's intention to pick him up. The prisoner's two sons, were standing by, but dared not interfere. Teddy Taylor then came rushing at George Jones, and the fight became general. The deceased came up then, swinging his arms about, and the prisoner said, 'One to one, no two's.' Taylor turned prisoner round and ran in and 'collared' George (Jones). Someone kicked prisoner from behind.

The prisoner said:

My son, George, shouted out, 'Oh.'

The prisoner then spoke very quietly, ending his next sentence in an almost inaudible voice:

That is when I struck.

The prisoner went on to say:

Two men were holding my son by the throat. I was knocked to the ground and several punches were rained on me. Ellis Lingard took hold of my ears, then took hold of my right hand as I was lying on the ground.

The prisoner denied using the dagger before the fight. The weapon was a relic of the war. He used to show it 'up and down in the pubs'. He said he put it in his pocket on Friday afternoon, but he had no particular reason for putting it there and he had it on his person during the whole of Saturday and on Sunday. The prisoner added that he had no grudge against the deceased. They had the last two pints together and the prisoner paid Taylor 1s 3d he owed him. They also played a game of darts:

Mr Grotrian: *You had no part in these quarrels before the stabbing?*
Prisoner: *No, sir. I did not wish to revenge myself on anybody.*
Mr Grotrian: *What made you think your son's life was in danger?*
Prisoner: *Two men had hold of him by the throat, and I thought he was being strangled to death. I know the parties. They reckon to cripple them and then give them £50 to keep them out of such places as this. My son could not speak the next day*
Mr Grotrian: *Do you think if you had not killed Taylor your son would have been killed?*
Prisoner: *Yes, and I thought two or three others of my sons would have been crippled or killed.*
Mr Grotrain: *Do you tell the jury that it was necessary instantly to kill Taylor to save your son's life?*
Prisoner: *I did not take that into consideration.*
Mr Grotrain: *Surely Mr Jones, you must have been feeling something along those lines.*
Prisoner: *Yes.*

The prisoner denied saying that it looked like murder, or that someone was going to get it. He said it looked like someone being killed. He did not know the dagger was in his pocket. Mr Grotrain asked the prisoner why he did not put his arms around Taylor instead of striking him with a dagger, to which the prisoner replied that he was a more helpless cripple than a little child. He did not know he had struck the deceased twice until the inquest.

The prisoner's eldest son, Thomas Jones, said he also thought that George Jones was in danger of being strangled. Amos Jones caused some amusement when he entered the witness box, following him saying:

When I comes out of the public house and got hit in the mouth, I says in my own mind, 'Tha will have to shake thysen up a bit Amos. It looks like being a bit hot.'

The case came to an abrupt conclusion on Tuesday 24 March, following the evidence of a large number of defence witnesses.

Mark Jones, one of the prisoner's sons, said,

Teddy Taylor rushed up to George Jones exclaiming, 'I'll – well kill thee.' Teddy Taylor struck George twice. Edward Dyson was running around getting kicks in where he could. Ellis Lingard was twisting my Dads ears enough to twist them off.

George Jones, another son of the prisoner, told how his father had come to his assistance when he was being held by the throat. According to James Benjamin Woods, miner, of 25 Elliott's Terrace, Wombwell, the prisoner was in the habit of carrying the dagger around. It was 'as sharp as a needle', and a very dangerous weapon, fashioned like a small sword bayonet. Another witness referred to the fight as a riot; and a thirteen-year-old schoolboy, Harold Thackeray, of East View, Wombwell, described how he had seen the prisoner and five sons walking to Dyson's house, and Edward Dyson take a running kick at the prisoner. Frank Arnold Jones, of 6 Staniforth Road, Wombwell (no relation to the prisoner), gave similar evidence to the schoolboy, adding that Walter Taylor struck George Jones three times in the face. Fred Greasley, a woodcutting machinist, also of Wombwell, said, he saw Walter Taylor attack George Jones and strike him in the mouth. Later he noticed George Jones bending backwards and the man had his knuckles on his windpipe. As he was walking away, having had enough, he heard someone cry out:

They've done him.

Mr Greasley said he thought they were referring to the man being strangled.

It was the opinion of witness Frank Allen, of Elliott's Terrace, Wombwell, that when George Jones delivered the fatal blow, he, the prisoner, was in danger of being strangled. Other witnesses came forward with similar evidence, and after no fewer than eighteen witnesses had been called for the defence, Mr Gretorian said:

> *I realize that I cannot ask the jury to find the prisoner guilty of wilful murder, but I will press very strongly for a verdict of manslaughter. I realize there was great provocation, so I am prepared to withdraw the charge of murder. I understand that in the circumstances that defence will plead guilty to the charge of manslaughter.*

Mr W P Donald, for the defence, said:

> *I have felt throughout that I could not carry on the defence to its full extent. I feel sure that there was much on both sides, as well as in the state of the community from which these men come, that is reprehensible. I have advised my client to plead guilty to manslaughter. I would like to take this opportunity to emphasize my client's previous good character and to stress that his intervention was as a peacemaker and not as a creator trouble.*

In summing up, Mr Justice Branson said:

> *. . . It would have been impossible in the ordinary way for me to take a light view of the case but taking into consideration the fact that the prisoner had gone as peacemaker, and not as attacker, I find it possible to be much more lenient than I otherwise would have been. To attack a man with a knife is nevertheless a serious offence and I cannot do less than pass a sentence of less than twelve months' imprisonment.*

The sentence was received with audible satisfaction in the Court. Jones received the verdict impassively, maintaining the attitude of dejected indifference, an air he had adopted throughout the trial.

Sources and Further Reading

Newspapers

The Times: 6 October 1834; 11 February 1874; 1, 11 September 1888; 14 December 1889; 1 January 1890; 21 December 1923.

Barnsley Chronicle and Penistone, Wath and Hoyland Journal: 14, 21, 28 December 1867; 11 January 1868; 1, 8, 22 February 1868; 4 April 1868; 15 September 1888; 22 December 1888.

Barnsley Chronicle & South Yorkshire News: 29 July 1933; 22 April 1939; 6 September 1947.

Barnsley Independent: 1 March 1884; 5 August 1892; 28 January 1905; 7 June 1919; 10 November 1923; 15 December 1923; 21 February 1925; 28 March 1925.

The Barnsley Times and General Advertiser, and Record of Mining and Manufacturing Interests: 25 May 1855; 21 July 1855; 14 December 1867; 11, 18 January 1868; 1, 8, 22 February 1868; 4 April 1868.

The Barnsley Times and South Yorkshire Gazette: 25 March 1871; 13 February 1875; 16 January 1875, 10 July 1875.

Sheffield and Rotherham Independent: 18, 19 December 1868; 2, 21 February 1869; 25, 26, 29 March 1869; 11 April 1878; 15 February 1889; 14 December 1889; 1 January 1890; 18, 22 September 1922; 2, 21 December 1922; 24 August 1893; 1892; 19, 20, 21, 22, 23, 24 August.

South Yorkshire Times and Express/Mexborough and Swinton Times: 10 February 1882; 6 May 1898; 11 January 1908; 8 January 1910; 5 March 1910; 4 January 1913; 19 April 1913; 1 February 1919; 13 July 1900; 20 July 1900; 22 July 1922; 12 February 1926; 15 April 1927.

Doncaster Chronicle: 15 February 1867; 5 April 1867; 31 May 1867.

The Illustrated Police News: 4 November 1876.

Star: 16, 18, 19, 21, 22 September 1922.

Sheffield Daily Telegraph: 19, 20, 22, 24 August 1889; 14 December 1889; 1 January 1889; 23 September 1922; 2 December 1922; 5, 6 January 1923.

Books

The Sheffield Murders 1865–1965, David Bentley, 2003 (ALD Design & Print, Sheffield).

Potters' Corner, Ken Wyatt, 2005 (AMS Educational).

Index